HOW DO I DECIDE?

A CONTEMPORARY JEWISH APPROACH TO WHAT'S RIGHT AND WHAT'S WRONG

ROLAND B. GITTELSOHN

BEHRMAN HOUSE, INC., PUBLISHERS

WEST ORANGE, NEW JERSEY

To our grandchildren
in the hope that
these pages will help them
make important decisions

The editor and publisher gratefully acknowledge the cooperation of the following sources of photographs for this book:

Animals Animals, 106; Bill Aron, 4, 6 (both), 11, 33 (both), 41, 51, 58 (top right), 63, 68, 69 (top left), 79 (top right), 80, 89 (both), 91 (top left; right), 94 (bottom), 99, 101 (both), 107, 112, 114, 121 (top), 122 (bottom), 145, 156 (bottom), 160 (bottom), 161 (both), 163 (top left; bottom right); Bettmann Archive, 135 (top); FPG International, ii (Mike Valeri), 3 (Renaud Thomas), 21 (Gary Holland Gibson), 23 (Richard Nowitz), 24 (Robert J. Bennett), 27 (top, Carolyn A. McKeone), 31 (Richard Nowitz), 48, 53, 58 (bottom), 76 (top, Alan Oddie), 79 (bottom right, Jonathan A. Meyers), 83, 93, 122 (top, Renaud Thomas), 143 (both), 146 (Jonathan A. Myers), 147 (Jeffrey W. Myers), 157; Gamma Liaison, 27 (bottom, Göksin Sipahioglu), 56 (top, Michael Abramson); Globe Photos, 17 (Horst Schafer), 25, 26, 29 (Hendrik Jan Van Brandwijk), 36, 45 (J.-P. Fizet), 64 (top, Tom Blau), 66 (top, Jon Blau), 69 (top right, Horst Schafer), 76 (bottom, Michel Giannoulatos), 86, 97, 120, 133, 153 (Mahler), 159, 163 (top right, Horst Schafer), 163 (bottom left, Colin Davey), 165; Granger Collection, 5, 7, 43, 50, 58 (top left), 65, 70, 78, 95 (top left; bottom), 105, 134 (bottom), 137 (both), 141, 142; Historical Pictures Service, 52, 95 (top left), 119: Magnum, 12 (Eugene Richards), 13 (Eugene Richards), 14 (Eugene Richards), 18 (Paul Fusco), 19 (Paul Fusco), 32 (Paul Fusco), 38 (Leonard Freed), 49 (both, Bruce Davidson), 73 (Alex Webb), 88 (Wayne Miller), 91 (bottom left, Richard Kalvar), 94 (top, Ian Berry), 113 (Ferdinando Scianna), 117 (Alex Webb), 131, 155 (bottom right, Bruce Davidson); New York Times, 151; Photo Researchers, 66 (bottom, Barbara Rios), 67 (Richard Hutchings), 69 (bottom left, Christa Armstrong; bottom right, Ulrike Welsch), 72 (Roberta Hershenson), 74 (top, George Whiteley; bottom, Arthur Tress), 79 (bottom left, Renee Lynn), 84 (Jan Lukas), 87 (Bruce Roberts), 100 (top, Bill Aron; bottom, Kenneth Murray), 109 (Blair Seitz), 118 (F. B. Grunzweig), 121 (bottom, Bill Aron), 126 (Barbara Rios), 134 (top, Roy Ellis), 136 (Bruce Roberts), 144 (Barbara Rios), 155 (top; bottom left, Spencer C. Grant III), 160 (top, Eugene Gordon); Superstock, front cover; Sygma, 15 (L'Illustration/Sygma), 22 (J.P. Laffont), 28 (Allan Tannenbaum), 35 (Douglas Kirkland), 44 (both, William Karel); 47 (Alain DeJean), 54 (both, Janet Knott/Boston Globe), 56 (bottom), 75 (J.P. Laffont), 77, 79 (top left, Tony Korody), 110 (top, Ira Wyman; bottom, Pierre Laffont), 115 (Tannenbaum), 123 (Michel Philippot), 124 (top, Brian Reynolds; bottom, Fineman), 139 (Tannenbaum), 152 (top, Patty Wood; bottom, David Woo/Dallas Morning News), 156 (top left, Tannenbaum; top right, Jean-Louis Atlan); UN Photo, 135 (bottom); Wide World, 34 (both).

Behrman House, Inc., Publishers
235 Watchung Avenue
West Orange, N.J. 07052

Designer: Binns & Lubin/Martin Lubin
Project Editor: Geoffrey Horn

Library of Congress Cataloging-in-Publication Data

Gittelsohn, Roland Bertram, 1910–

How do I decide? : a contemporary Jewish approach to what's right and what's wrong / Roland B. Gittelsohn.

p.   cm.

Summary: Draws on the Jewish tradition to advise adolescents on making ethical decisions about death, family, sex, and other areas of life.

ISBN 0-87441-488-1 : $8.95

1. Ethics, Jewish—Juvenile literature.   2. Conduct of life—Juvenile literature.   [1. Ethics, Jewish.   2. Conduct of life.   3. Decision making.]   I. Title.

BJ1285.G55   1989

296.7'4—dc20

89-6849
CIP
AC

CONTENTS

Beginnings

CHAPTER ONE

WHAT TO EXPECT

What would you point to as the most pressing ethical problem you face today?

- Struggling to assert your independence without rejecting your parents?

- Resisting pressure from your peers to experiment with alcohol or drugs?

- Reconciling the ideals you have been taught at home and in religious school with the corruption so evident in the worlds of politics and business?

- Trying to decide whether and when it's right to tell a lie rather than the truth?

- Dealing with your parents' insistence that you date only Jews?

- Coping with your emerging sexuality and wondering how you can express it without endangering your principles, your health, or your future?

These problems and others are especially compelling to people your age. You have already outgrown many of the values and standards of childhood but are still in the process of developing adult ideals.

Are the problems you face today more complex than those your parents and grandparents confronted as adolescents?

This may be a difficult period for you—more difficult for you, in fact, than it was for your parents and grandparents. So much has changed since they were adolescents. The threat of nuclear war, the exploration of space, the emergence of new experimental patterns in family and sexual behavior, the ability to prolong life by artificial means—these are but a few of the exciting, sometimes frightening changes that combine to make the ethical challenges confronting you more difficult than those that faced any previous generation.

In working out your own answers to these vexing ethical dilemmas, you will often be able to find adult role models that are helpful. The words—and even more important, the deeds—of parents, teachers, rabbis, camp counselors, coaches, and community and national leaders can give you wise guidance. You are not limited, however, to living models.

Drawing on the past

This book grows out of my lifelong conviction that the Jewish tradition can also offer you significant assistance. Our Jewish heritage has been developing for about four thousand years. From our collective experience during these forty centuries have come many insights, values, and truths that are still uniquely valid.

In some cases you will find direct help from our heritage in confronting your problems. More often you will have to extrapolate—that is, identify the principles established by tradition, then use your own intelligence and conscience in applying these principles to your dilemma. For obvious reasons, you will find nothing in ancient, medieval, or pre-modern Judaism regarding nuclear war. But the tradition does have important things to

Do you accept uncritically what your teachers say? Your textbooks? Your parents? Your friends?

4

The first hydrogen bomb blast at Enewetak (1952).

How have science and technology made your world different from the world your great-grandparents knew?

say about respect for human life and property in the waging of war, whether conventional or nuclear. The bridge between traditional wisdom and contemporary behavior is one you have to construct. In each case, you will need to ask how our past authorities would most probably have decided the matter if, in addition to their wisdom, they had our knowledge of history and science.

Because most Orthodox Jews believe that everything contained in the Bible and

Talmud emanates from God and is therefore immutable, they tend to resist adaptation and change. Progressive Jews—Conservative, Reconstructionist, and Reform—are convinced to one degree or another that our tradition, although inspired by God, has come down to us through fallible men and women and must therefore be reinterpreted by each generation of fallible men and women. In evaluating tradition, we have three choices:

1. We may decide that the guidance our authorities originally provided remains valid and should be followed without change.

Torah and Talmud: what light can they shed on the ethical dilemmas you face today?

2. We may conclude, in the light of subsequent knowledge and moral development, that this guidance is no longer relevant and must therefore be discarded.

3. We may resolve that the guidance our authorities gave us is still valid in principle but, because of changed circumstances, must now be reinterpreted and adapted.

I am profoundly convinced that no part of our Jewish ethical tradition should be either accepted or rejected until it has been carefully understood and evaluated. My purpose in these pages is to help you do exactly that.

Looking toward the future

This book is intended not to give you conclusive answers but to stimulate your own thinking. Each chapter presents examples and situations based on real problems that confront many Jewish young people in the United States and Canada today. I know these problems are real because, in choosing them, I surveyed several hundred high school students and youth advisers. The photographs in each chapter are intended not only to illustrate the problems but also to encourage you to think about them.

Each chapter also offers relevant selections from various categories of Jewish literature: Torah, Bible, Talmud, folk tales, Ḥasidic stories, and rulings by various rabbinic authorities, both ancient and modern. You are invited to examine these readings in order to decide what light they shed on the problems the chapter poses. To learn more about the source of a particular selection and to understand the relationship of the various texts to each other, refer to the Glossary on pages 168-169.

Finally, each chapter includes numerous questions for discussion and deliberation. Sometimes, as you review the readings and questions, a consensus on a problem may emerge. At other times, a significant difference of opinion may remain. I do give some of my own views, not in the expectation that you will accept them unthinkingly but in the hope that they will prod your own thinking. I may be wrong in some of my conclusions. You too may be wrong. What matters is that we discuss these problems in the light of Jewish tradition and that we continue to think deeply about them even after we have reached what seem to be reasonable conclusions. Even more important is that after we have thoroughly examined and tested our conclusions, we try consistently to act on them.

We have many exciting moments of thinking and discussing ahead of us. Let us learn from each other and from centuries of Jewish tradition. Let us respect even those with whom we disagree vigorously. And together, let us wisely use the past to plan the future.

Yom Kippur at a New York City synagogue (1871).

How does this scene differ from what you might see in your own temple on the High Holy Days? What Jewish objects and symbols remain the same? Why does Judaism need both continuity and change in order to survive as a way of life?

Life and Death

CHAPTER TWO

WHAT'S KIND? WHAT'S CRUEL?

Difficult choices

Lois and Fred Roth had always felt very close to their grandparents. When the twins were young, Gram and Gramp spent a lot of time with them, often took them to parks and zoos, always brought them delightful gifts from their trips.

But now, Gram has developed Alzheimer's disease, a serious brain affliction that is destroying her memory and makes it impossible for her to perform independently even such simple daily tasks as washing and dressing. Gramp, who has a heart condition, is no longer able to take care of her by himself.

The Roth family has spent many agonizing evenings discussing what to do. Should they close up the elderly couple's apartment and bring them into their own home? Or should they try to find a good nursing home where Gram and Gramp can be together and where professional help and medical services will be available?

Has your family ever had to make a choice like the one facing the Roths? What were the options available to you? What were the advantages and disadvantages of each? Which option did your family choose? In general, whose welfare should be given priority in making such a choice: (a) the grandchildren's, (b) their parents', or (c) their grandparents'?

Imagine yourself seventy years from now, living on your own in a house or apartment. When you are no longer able to care for yourself, where will you live? With your grown children? In a retirement community? In a nursing home?

Caring

Do not cast me off in old age; when my strength fails, do not forsake me!

Psalms 71:9

An old person who has forgotten his or her learning because of the ravages of age is to be treated with the reverence due the holy ark . . . which, in later days, after the tablets had been lost, was also empty but still honored.

Jerusalem Mo'ed Katan 3:1

Each of these passages refers specifically to old age and its infirmities. To what extent might they also apply to youthful sufferers from AIDS? Crime victims? The homeless? What attitude should we take toward those whose lives have been blighted by misfortune?

The disciples of Rabbi Eliezer the Great asked him to give an example of honoring one's parents. He said, "Go and see what Dama ben Netinah did in Ashkelon. His mother was feeble-minded and she used to strike him with a shoe in the presence of the council over which he presided, but he never said more than, 'It is enough, Mother.' After the shoe fell from her hand, he would pick it up for her so she would not be troubled.

Jerusalem Peah 1:1

How did Dama ben Netinah avoid humiliating his mother in public? What does this story show about the kind of person he was? For which Roth family option might this story be taken as evidence: bringing Gram and Gramp into the home, or placing them in an institution?

Testing for Alzheimer's disease.

Can you imagine what your life would be like if you were unable to perform even such simple tasks as washing and dressing without assistance?

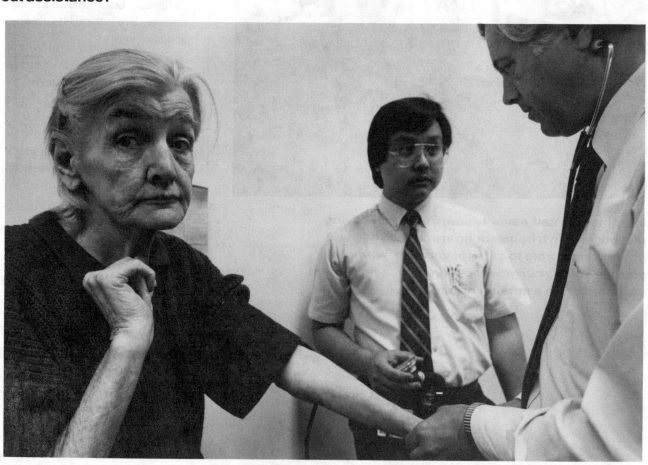

Responsibilities of others

If the mind of his father or his mother is affected, the son should make every effort to indulge the vagaries of the stricken parent until God will have mercy on the afflicted.

But if the condition of the parent has grown worse, and the son is no longer able to endure the strain, he may leave his father or mother, go elsewhere, and delegate others to give the proper care.

Maimonides, Laws Concerning Rebels, *6:10*

Have you ever had a chronically ill grandparent (or other relative) living in your home? What strains did that impose on the household? What do you think Maimonides meant by the phrase ''until God will have mercy on the afflicted''?

In earlier years there was no place for a parent who was failing in health to be taken care of except in the family home. . . . Now there are homes for the aged with hospital facilities. . . . If these institutions are well conducted by responsible people, there is no question that the old person can be taken care of (at least from the physical point of view) much better than . . . at home. But the difficulty is psychological or emotional. Often . . . the parent does not wish to leave the home of his dear ones . . . and his or her unwillingness to go must be counted as at least one element in [the decision].

S. Freehof, New Reform Responsa *(Hebrew Union College Press, 1980), pp. 93ff*

Returning to the example of the Roth family, what if Gram and Gramp refused to move out of their apartment? How much pressure should other family members exert in order to get them to move? Suppose, in addition to their concerns about Gram's medical needs, the Roths were worried about the rising crime rate

Where should this Alzheimer's victim and her husband live when he is no longer strong enough to provide for her daily needs?

and declining services in the grandparents' neighborhood? What steps would they be justified in taking to move the grandparents to a better location?

Notice that the Freehof passage refers to institutions that are ''well conducted by responsible people.'' How can the Roth family ensure that the nursing home it chooses for Gram and Gramp fits that description? What can the Roths do to make sure the nursing home remains ''well conducted'' after Gram and Gramp move there? What can your temple—and your class—do to help nursing homes cater to the spiritual and psychological as well as the physical needs of their residents?

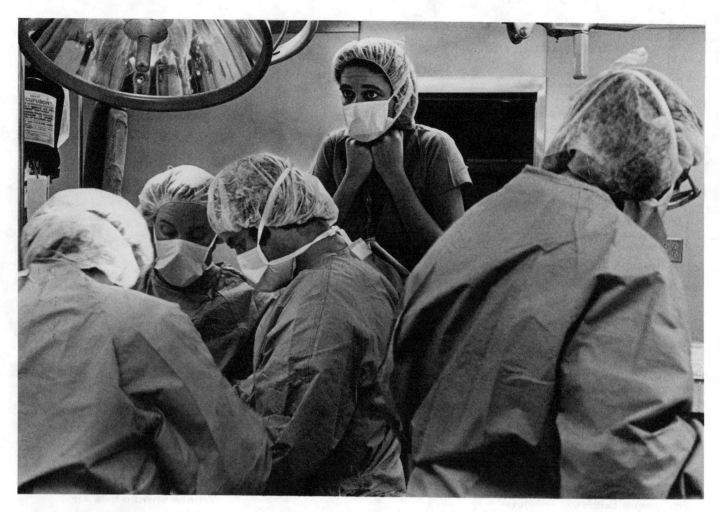

When are doctors and nurses required to do all they can to save a patient's life? When are they permitted to stop "heroic measures" and let death take its course?

Desperate measures

Now suppose Grandma Roth's condition has deteriorated to the point where she is totally unaware of herself or her surroundings. She recognizes no one, not even her husband. Her only nutrition is through a nasal tube, which, even though she appears to be unconscious, she regularly rips out of her nose.

Her doctors have asked for permission to insert a feeding tube surgically through her abdomen. This would not restore her to consciousness or improve her condition in any way, although it would prevent her from starving. Without it, she will most probably die within a month. What should be done? Who has the ultimate responsibility for making this choice: Grandpa Roth? The entire Roth family? The surgeons? The hospital's board of medical ethics?

Euthanasia

The word *euthanasia*, which comes from Greek, literally means "a good death." It commonly refers to a deliberate human act that causes or permits death to a seriously ill patient. If Grandma Roth's physicians were to inject into her vein a lethal drug, that would be *active euthanasia*. If they were simply to refrain from surgically inserting an abdominal feeding tube, that would be *passive euthanasia*.

Concerned as they were with the sanctity of life, our authorities dealt extensively with the question of whether the death of a terminally ill patient may be hastened in any way. From the selections that follow, can you tell what distinction, if any, our tradition makes between active and passive euthanasia? Does either form of euthanasia accord with traditional Jewish attitudes toward life and human dignity?

A right to life

One who kills a healthy or a dying person, or even a hopelessly sick man, is guilty of murder.

Maimonides, Hilkhot Rotzeaḥ *2:7*

If a person with only a few moments to live were to be considered less valuable than one with many years of life ahead, the value of every human being loses its absolute character. It becomes relative to life expectancy, to state of health, to intelligence, or usefulness to society, or to any other arbitrary criterion. . . . The erosion of the moral ethic begins when the nearly-dead are equated with the dead; this value judgment is then extended to encompass the inferior individual, the mentally retarded, the disabled or the incurably ill. The undesirable, the unproductive, or the alien are then also excluded from their inalienable right to life.

D. Feldman and F. Rosner, Compendium on Medical Ethics *(Federation of Jewish Philanthropies of New York, 1984), p. 13*

Rabbi Feldman and Dr. Rosner might well have had the Nazis in mind when they wrote this paragraph. Hitler ordered that all kinds of bizarre medical experiments be carried out on those he considered physically or mentally defective, especially the Jews. When the experiments were finished, those who had not already died were summarily executed.

Do you feel that legalizing active euthanasia might increase the risk of Nazi-like cruelties in this country? Could the same argument against active euthanasia also be made against abortion? If not, why not? If the Roths were to refuse their

surgeon permission to operate on Grandma, would that put them in the same category as the Nazis?

On the third day, a man came from Saul's camp. . . . David said to him, "Where are you coming from?" He answered, "I have just escaped from the camp of Israel." "What happened?" asked David. "Tell me!" And he told him how the troops had fled the battlefield, and that, moreover, many of the troops had fallen and died; also that Saul and his son Jonathan were dead. "How do you know," David asked the young man who brought him the news, "that Saul and his son Jonathan are dead?" The young man

Treating a cholera victim in the 1880s.

How has medicine advanced since the nineteenth century? What new problems does such medical progress pose?

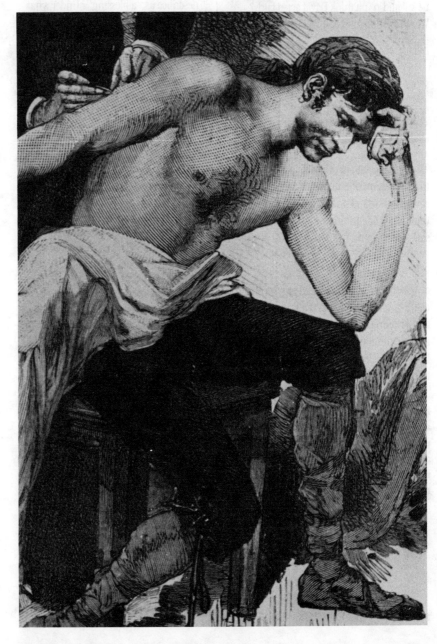

who brought in the news answered, ". . . I saw Saul leaning on his spear, and chariots and horsemen closing in on him. He looked around and saw me, and he called to me. . . . Then he said to me, 'Stand over me, and finish me off, for I am in agony and barely alive.' So I stood over him and finished him off, for I knew that he would never rise from where he was lying. . . ."

"How did you dare," David said to him, "to lift your hand and kill the Lord's anointed?" Thereupon David called one of the attendants and said to him, "Come over and strike him!" He struck him down and he died.

II Samuel 1:2-15

Why did David order that the messenger be killed? Do you think David acted fairly? Was the young man justified in complying with Saul's request?

A time for dying

Thus far, the answer of Jewish authority to the question of euthanasia seems absolutely clear and unambiguous. But the tradition is not quite so one-sided. Consider, for example, the response of Chayim Palaggi, chief rabbi of Smyrna in the mid-nineteenth century, to the question of whether it is permissible to pray for the death of a woman who is incurably ill and suffering terrible pain. After asserting that ordinarily it is forbidden to pray for anyone's death, Rabbi Palaggi continues:

But here, where she wishes it herself and can no longer endure her pain, it is possible to say that . . . it is permitted to ask mercy for a very sick person that he may die, so that his soul may come to rest. . . .

Why did Ecclesiastes say. "There is a time for dying"? It means that, when the time comes for a man's soul to go forth, people should not cry aloud that his soul shall return, for he can live only a short time and in that short time he must bear great pain.

Chayim Palaggi, responsum in Hikelei Lev, *1:50*

Why is it ordinarily forbidden to pray for anyone's death? Why is Rabbi Palaggi willing to allow an exception in this case? Why didn't the rabbi simply urge the questioner to pray for a miracle? Doesn't God have the power to accomplish anything—even the recovery of someone thought to be incurably ill?

Have you ever heard someone's death described as "a blessing"? Under what circumstances might death be considered a blessing?

If a person has reached the "age of strength" [eighty years], a sudden death is like dying from a kiss.

Mo'ed Katan 28a

How might a sudden death in old age be like "dying from a kiss"? What kind of death scene did the author of this passage envision? How does that scene differ from what Grandma Roth has experienced?

[W]e do encounter several modern authorities who take a more lenient view of passive euthanasia. Prominent among these is Rabbi Moshe Feinstein . . . [who] states that it is forbidden to maintain the life of a person "who is not fit to live" by artificial means. Discussing a situation in which doctors wish to maintain such a person on machines so as to use his organs in a transplant, he states that because the intention of such a course of action is not to heal the patient but merely to prolong his life for a time, then if the time thus gained by artificial means is characterized by pain and suffering for the patient, it would be forbidden. . . .

Rabbi I. Jakobovitz . . . concludes that there is no obligation to extend the life of a terminally ill patient, and thereby to perpetuate his pain artificially. He thus permits the removal of medication and treatment—but not of the natural means of subsistence, such as food and water.

Basil F. Herring, Jewish Ethics and Halakhah for Our Time *(Ktav/Yeshiva University Press, 1984), pp. 84f*

What real difference is there between withholding medication from a dying patient and withholding food? Can you conceive of any situation in which active euthanasia would be more merciful than passive euthanasia? How do you think today's rabbis should react to such a situation?

Knowing when to stop

It is . . . clear that we must use any medicine or drug which may help an individual. . . . However, these injunctions were modified with a dying individual (*gosais*) in the throes of death. In that case, it was considered appropriate for an individual to stop praying for the lives of those dear to him or pray for their release. . . . Furthermore, it was thought appropriate to stop acts which would hinder a soul from departure, so Sefer Chasidim (723) stated that if a dying person was disturbed by wood chopping, it should be halted so that the soul might depart peacefully. Isserles . . . stated that anything which stood in the way of peaceful death should be removed. . . . Clearly, as long as some form of independent life persists, nothing should be done to hasten death and all medicines which may be helpful must be used. Once this point has been passed, it is no longer necessary to utilize further medical devices in the form of drugs or mechanical apparatus.

Central Conference of American Rabbis, Committee on Responsa, American Reform Responsa *(CCAR 1983), p. 272*

Physically and mentally handicapped women raise money
for the Mothers March on Birth
Defects.

**Should doctors make every
effort to extend the lives of
all disabled newborns? Or
should some severely
handicapped infants be
allowed to die?**

In a "living will," a parent or grandparent requests in advance to be allowed to die if he or she becomes terminally ill and mentally unable to make such a decision. What do you think of such a "living will"? What would be the attitude of the Jewish authorities we have previously examined? If Grandma Roth had made a living will, would the burden of decision imposed on the Roth family and her physicians be any easier?

Worth the struggle?

Franz Rosenzweig was one of the most eminent philosophers and Bible translators of the early twentieth century. Early in life he suffered a rare disease that caused paralysis to encroach upon his

body inch by inch, until he was finally able to move only one finger. In order to write, he had to point—slowly, laboriously, painfully—to one letter at a time, while a companion transcribed his thoughts into words and sentences, then paragraphs and pages. In this way, Rosenzweig continued to work for many years. Few scholars in this century contributed more than he did to Jewish knowledge.

Suppose, because the outlook was so bleak, someone had suggested that Rosenzweig be allowed to die shortly after his disease was diagnosed. What would have been gained or lost? In what ways, if any, does his case differ from Grandma Roth's?

Competing values

Few questions we will consider in this book are more difficult than the ones posed in this chapter. They are difficult because they involve equally valid but competing values, and because for most thinking modern Jews there are no answers that are right or wrong under all circumstances. Consider the following cases:

1. A widow whose husband had just died was loudly lamenting her loss. Her rabbi pointed out to her that if her husband had not died, he would have been permanently paralyzed and comatose, recognizing no one, conscious of nothing. "I wouldn't care," the woman protested tearfully. "I'd rather have him with me that way than not at all!"

Was the rabbi right in what he said to her? Can we blame her for responding as she did? How do you think you would feel if you were in her situation?

2. Another woman, whose husband was being kept alive only by medical machinery, was asked by her doctors for permission to "pull the plug." They said there was absolutely no hope that her husband would ever recover or regain consciousness. "When God is ready for Jack, He'll take him. I'm not going to be the one to cause his death!"

What do you think of this woman's reaction? How would you answer her? Who should bear the cost of Jack's continued treatment? The woman? The hospital? The general public through increases in taxes or medical insurance rates? If a hospital has a limited number of physicians, beds, and medical supplies, who most deserves treatment: (a) Jack, (b) an incurably ill child, (c) a person of any age with a curable condition, (d) all patients equally? If you chose a, b, or c, does this mean you regard the other patients as "less valuable"?

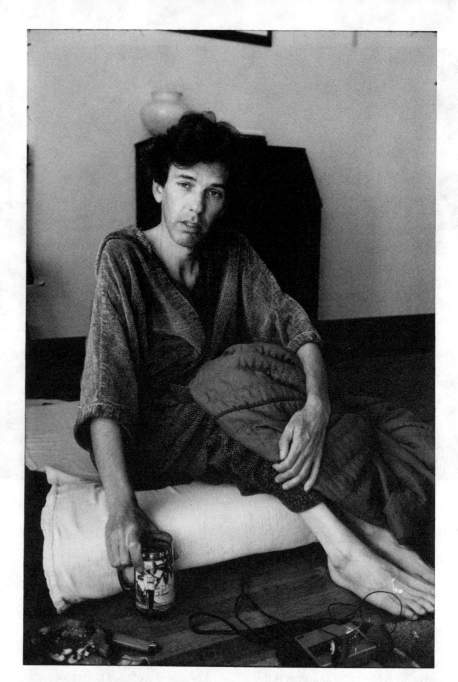

Does an AIDS sufferer have any greater or lesser right to medical care than a ninety-year-old man in an irreversible coma? Than an eight-year-old girl with a broken leg? Than a corporate president who needs heart bypass surgery? Who must pay for the care each receives?

A hospice—a special facility for the terminally ill.

What are the special physical and emotional needs of the terminally ill? What are the advantages and disadvantages of treating a terminally ill patient at home? In a hospital? In a hospice? Do people who take care of the terminally ill have special emotional needs? What, if anything, can others do to ease their burden?

How long?

Underlying this entire discussion is an incontestable premise: the sanctity of human life must be inviolate. But what, specifically, does this mean?

In 1975, when my first wife began nearly six years of hospitalization leading to her death, a good friend of ours had already been a patient at Jewish Memorial Hospital in Boston for three years. Biologically, that friend was still alive in 1988. But neither in 1975 nor thirteen years later was she in any way aware of herself or her surroundings. She could not recognize me as her rabbi. Nor could she recognize her husband or either of her sons. Medically, moreover, there was no hope for recovery or even improvement.

Is she still fully human? Does she reflect the image of God? Can her life still be considered sacred? Is she even, in any true sense of the word, alive?

It seems to me that a minimal first step is to accept the new definition of death by brain death or irreversible coma. These are tests which the medical profession can easily and definitely make. If we learn to accept death in such terms, some families will be spared the guilt and confusion which overwhelm them now when a doctor says, "Should I try everything that can be done?"... Children do no kindness to an elderly parent when they look at the doctor pleadingly and say, "Do everything you can do." For whom? For what? Often the answer is simply because we need to assuage our guilt....

It's one thing to fight for the life of a twenty-year-old whose life lies before him if there's the least chance he may regain consciousness and quite another to fight over the body of an eighty-eight-year-old whose physical strength is minimal and whose future is paralysis....

The brain is the human being. We die when the brain goes. That's when the soul leaves the body. To keep a vegetable alive is to keep a vegetable alive and nothing more.

Rabbi Daniel J. Silver in Jack Riemer (ed.), Jewish Reflections on Death *(Schocken, 1974), pp. 123f*

Do you agree with Rabbi Silver? Why or why not? If you feel that "brain death or irreversible coma" is not the right way to judge whether a person is dead, can you propose an alternative way of deciding? How might earlier Jewish authorities have responded to Rabbi Silver's claim that "when the brain goes" is "when the soul leaves the body"?

CHAPTER THREE

WHEN ENOUGH IS TOO MUCH

Peer pressure

Carla is troubled. At first it didn't particularly bother her that she was the only one in her crowd who didn't use alcohol or drugs. Of course, she'd had a few beers with her friends, but she didn't particularly like the taste. She'd also tried marijuana once or twice, but she didn't really enjoy it, so she stopped. When the gang added cocaine to their weekend routine, she just made excuses not to join them.

Carla knows they think she's no fun to be with, but she doesn't think what they do is so much fun, either. On the other hand, she doesn't want to lose her friends.

Surrounded by drinkers and smokers, it's hard to resist the pressure to join in. What answers can you give friends who push you to try beer and cigarettes—or drugs—when you really don't want to?

Against drinking

Drink no wine or ale, you or your sons with you, when you enter the tent of meeting, that you may not die—it is a law for all time throughout your generations—for you must distinguish between the sacred and the profane, and between the unclean and the clean.

Leviticus 10:9-10

Wine is a scoffer, strong drink a roisterer; He who is muddled by them will not grow wise.

Proverbs 20:1

Do not be of those who guzzle wine,
Or glut themselves on meat;
For guzzlers and gluttons will be
    impoverished,
And drowsing will clothe you in tatters.

Proverbs 23:30-21

Some people have cited Scripture to support their opposition to the drinking of all alcoholic beverages. Are they justified in doing so? Does the selection from Leviticus ban all drinking—or only the drinking of wine or ale at a particular time and place? Does the author of Proverbs contend that all drinking is harmful—or only the kind of excessive drinking that muddles the mind and gluts the senses?

Are Jews who manufacture, sell, or advertise alcoholic beverages committing an immoral act? What responsibility, if any, do those who promote the use of alcohol bear for the toll that alcoholism takes on individuals, families, and society as a whole? What responsibility, if any, do they bear for the injuries and deaths that are caused by drunk driving? Do you believe that those who make, sell, or advertise beer and other alcoholic drinks have a special responsibility to reduce the damage their products cause? If so, what steps should the liquor industry take in educating people to use alcohol wisely?

What responsibility, if any, do people who promote the use of alcohol bear for the destructive social effects of alcohol abuse?

Between 1920 and 1933, the sale and consumption of alcoholic beverages, except for medicinal purposes, was prohibited by law in the United States. Was Prohibition an effective solution to the problem of drunkenness? Why was it repealed? How would you answer those who compare the outlawing of drugs in our own time to the failed policies of the Prohibition era?

In praise of wine

How can we reconcile the earlier warnings against alcohol with the blessing of wine during Kiddush? With the four cups of wine consumed during the Passover seder? With the adage that on Purim you should drink until you can't tell the difference between "cursed Haman" and "blessed Mordecai"?

You make the grass grow for the cattle,
   and herbage for man's labor
   that he may get food out of the
      earth—
   wine that cheers the hearts of men,
   oil that makes the face shine,
   and bread that sustains man's life.

Psalms 104:14-15.

When Noah went to plant a vineyard, Satan appeared before him.

"What are you planting?" asked Satan.

"A vineyard," answered Noah.

"What is it like?" asked Satan.

"Its fruits are always sweet, whether fresh or dry, and wine is made of them to gladden the heart," Noah replied.

"Let us form a partnership in this vineyard," Satan proposed.

"Very well," said Noah.

What did Satan do?

He brought a sheep and a lamb, and slew them under the vine.

Then he brought in turn a lion, a pig, and a monkey and slew each so that their blood dripped into the vineyard and drenched the soil.

In that way Satan hinted that before a person drinks wine he is simple like a sheep and quiet like a lamb.

When he has drunk in moderation, he is strong as a lion and thinks no one in the world is as strong as he.

When he has drunk more than enough, he becomes like a pig, wallowing in filth.

And when he is completely drunk, he makes a monkey of himself, dancing about, spewing out obscenities and unaware of anything he is doing.

Tanḥuma on Genesis, portion Noah, par. 13

What implication do you draw from the way the parable portrays Satan as a partner in Noah's vineyard? Does the comparison of a wine drinker with a lion, a pig, and a monkey correspond with your own observations of friends or relatives who have had too much to drink? How attractive does the parable make drunkenness look?

A Yemenite seder in Israel.

How do you reconcile some of the Bible's warnings against wine with the blessing of wine in the Kiddush and at the seder table?

Drunk driving

You have spent the evening at a friend's birthday party. Her parents weren't home, and the beer flowed freely for several hours. Despite your intention to remain sober, now that it's time to leave, neither you nor any of your companions is sober enough to drive safely.

Should you call a cab? Call your parents to tell them you're sleeping over? Ask your parents for a lift home? Or do you decide to drive home anyway, reasoning that the risk of driving drunk is preferable to what might happen if your parents find out you've been drinking? Suppose that instead of being the driver, you're a passenger in a car being driven by a drunken friend. What do you do now?

Running risks

Rabbi Nathan said, "Whence do we know that a man should not keep a vicious dog in his home, or keep an insecure ladder in his home? Because it is said, 'Thou shalt not bring blood upon thy house' (Deuteronomy 22:8)."

Baba Kamma 15b

What does the Torah mean in commanding people not to "bring blood" upon their houses? How might this phrase apply to drinking excessive amounts of alcohol? Driving drunk? Using drugs? Failing to supervise your children properly when they hold a party?

Rabbi Akiba said, "A man is not permitted to harm himself."

Mishnah Baba Kamma 90a

People between the ages of 16 and 24 make up about 18 percent of all licensed drivers but account for nearly 39 percent of all drunk driving deaths.

How would you stop someone you knew from driving home drunk?

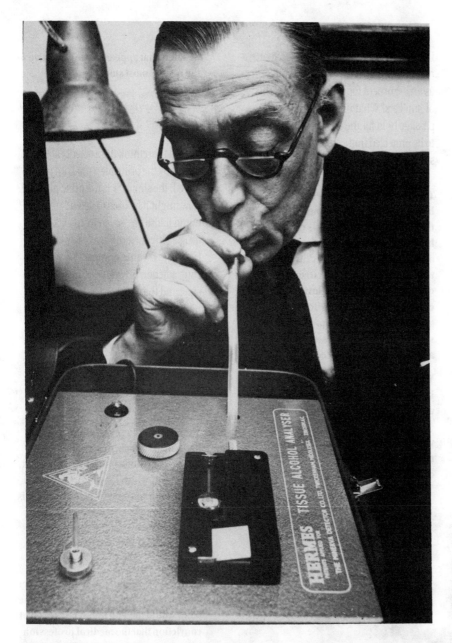

A breathalyzer test determines the amount of alcohol that has entered a driver's bloodstream.

Do you favor stiffer penalties for drunk drivers? How else might you reduce the threat that drunk drivers pose to themselves and others?

One should avoid all things that might lead to danger, because a danger to life is more serious than a prohibition, and one should be more concerned about a possible danger to life than a possible prohibition. Therefore the sages prohibited one to walk in a place of danger, such as near a leaning wall or alone at night. They also prohibited drinking water from rivers at night, or placing one's mouth on a flowing pipe of water to drink. For these things may lead to danger. . . . They also said that one should flee from a city where there is a plague, at the beginning of the outbreak. All these things are intended to avoid danger, and one who is concerned with his health will avoid them. And it is prohibited to rely on some saving miracle.

Rema, *commentary on Shulḥan Arukh,* Yoreh Day'ya *116:5*

Does the caution this passage offers about walking alone at night sound familiar to you? Are there places in your community where you try to avoid walking alone? What other risky behaviors do you try to avoid? What would the author of this passage say about mountain climbing, lion taming, or other feats of daring? Can appropriate training and precautions help reduce the risk? What does the author mean by warning that "it is prohibited to rely on some saving miracle"?

Suppose a thirty-eight-year-old tells you: "Look, I'm an adult. My body and my life are my own. If I want to take risks with my health, that's my business and no one else's. If I'm lucky, I'll have a good time. If I'm not lucky, I'm the only one who'll get hurt. Anyway, there's no guarantee that if I live carefully, I'll avoid all injury or pain." How do you respond? Is it true that when we harm ourselves, we're the only ones who suffer? What about our families? Friends? Colleagues?

Smoking

Carla has never seen her mother so angry. The firm she works for as a supervisor has just issued a new ruling that prohibits smoking anywhere in the building except in the lavatories. "What right do they have to dictate my life?" Mrs. Rogers demands. "It's bad enough the company has divided the cafeteria into smoking and nonsmoking sections. What right does the company have to tell me that the ladies' room is the only place I can relax with a cigarette? Don't smokers have rights, too?"

Smokestacks are to be removed from the city to a distance of fifty cubits.

Tosefta, Baba Batra 1:7

Do you think it's fair to use this ancient regulation governing industrial pollution as an argument for restricting the rights of smokers? What implications does this passage hold for the right of nonsmokers to be protected from "second-hand smoke"?

To summarize these approaches to tobacco, alcohol and non-medical drugs, the following emerges. It is clearly prohibited to shorten one's life, or deliberately harm one's health. . . . At the same time, and under certain circumstances, one may undertake certain activities that could be considered perilous on the grounds that "the Lord preserveth the simple" if such activities are widespread and a commonly accepted risk. . . .

When applied to the question of smoking tobacco, such considerations lead most authorities to a permissive stance. . . . On the other hand, the permissive view denies the immediate danger, and thereby is willing to rely on a measure of divine providence, and the margin

of safety that appears to be operative in the case of most smokers.

Basil F. Herring, Jewish Ethics and Halakhah for Our Time *(Ktav/Yeshiva University Press, 1984), pp. 237ff*

What do you think the ancient rabbis meant by the principle "the Lord preserveth the simple"? Is the principle valid? How might it be used to defend smoking? Could it also be used to justify taking drugs? Driving a car at excessive speeds? Having sex with a stranger? Do you see a contradiction between this rabbinic principle and the admonition that "it is prohibited to rely on some saving miracle"?

It is distinctly a duty incumbent upon every person to protect his health. The Mishnah, in Baba Kamma 8:6 (and the Talmud in 91b), states that a person may not injure himself. . . .

Therefore, if, for example, a man has had a heart attack, or has some lung infection or some other bodily ailment, because of which his physician orders him to stop smoking, it is not only ordinary caution for this man to obey his physician, but it may be considered a mandate of Jewish law that he should do so.

As for other people who smoke, whether Jewish law would have them give up the habit would depend upon the degree of conviction that the medical profession has come to with regard to it. If ever the medical profession definitely agrees that the use of tobacco is of danger to every human being, then, of course it could be argued that Jewish law, which commands self-preservation, would prohibit its use.

S. Freehof, Reform Responsa for Our Time *(Hebrew Union College Press, 1977), pp. 55f*

Do smokers have the right to smoke whenever and wherever they want? Do nonsmokers have the right to be protected from the hazards and annoyance of "second-hand smoke"?

Rabbi Solomon Freehof, in his 1977 responsum, seems to hesitate on the question of whether Jewish law prohibits smoking. What do you think his attitude would be today? Why?

Do you believe tobacco companies have a moral as well as a legal obligation to inform the public about the hazards of smoking? Should tobacco companies also be required to compensate smokers who develop health problems as a result of smoking? Or do you believe that smokers should bear all the responsibility for the risks they assume?

Drugs

Rav said to his son Ḥiyya, "Do not take drugs."

Pesaḥim 113a

Similarly, regarding any obstacle which is dangerous to life, there is a positive commandment to remove and beware of it, and to be particularly careful in this matter, for Scripture says, "Take heed unto thyself and guard thy soul diligently" (Deuteronomy 4:9). If one does not remove dangerous obstacles and allows them to remain, he disregards a positive commandment and transgresses the prohibition, "Bring no blood upon thy house" (Deuteronomy 22:8). Many things are forbidden by the sages because they are dangerous to life. If one disregards any of these and says, "If I want to put myself in danger, what concern is it to others," or "I am not particular about such things," disciplinary flogging is inflicted upon him.

Maimonides, Hilkhot Rotzeaḥ *11:4f*

Do you agree with Maimonides that the community has the right to discipline those who act in ways that threaten their own health and, potentially, the well-being of others? Do you favor arresting drug

What would you do if you found out your best friend was using crack or uppers and downers? Whom would you tell? How would you try to get your friend to stop?

What dangers do users of needle drugs pose to themselves and others?

users as well as sellers? Stiffer jail terms for drunk drivers? Fines for those who smoke in public places? Prison sentences or quarantine for AIDS sufferers who engage in unsafe sex?

Do not drink drugs, because they demand periodic doses, and your heart will crave them. You will waste much money thereby. Even for medical care do not drink them, and if possible obtain another mode of healing.

Maimonides, commentary on Mishnah Baba Kamma 90a

An eminent modern Orthodox authority, Rabbi Moshe Feinstein, specifically prohibits the smoking of marijuana:

In the first place, marijuana is harmful to bodily functions, whether physical or mental. . . . A second reason . . . is the problem of addiction, or at least "great longing" that makes it exceedingly dif-

ficult for one to be weaned from the habit. . . . A third reason for the prohibition is that the drug user . . . might well resort to violence against his fellows in order to obtain that which he craves.

Herring, Jewish Ethics, *pp. 237ff*

How do you interpret the term "great longing"? How does it differ from addiction? In general, which of Rabbi Feinstein's arguments do you consider valid? Which do you consider invalid? Why? Would his arguments persuade you not to try marijuana? Do you think they would convince most of your peers? If not, why not? Which arguments, if any, are most effective in persuading people not to use drugs? If you have ever been offered a drug, what reason did you give for saying no? What response did you receive?

Dealing with substance abuse

In what ways is the use of drugs similar to smoking cigarettes or drinking liquor? In what ways different? Would it be easier to say no to alcohol and tobacco if there were more laws restricting their use? Do you think you would find it more difficult to resist becoming dependent on drugs, alcohol, and tobacco if you were living in a college dormitory instead of at home with your parents? Why? To what extent do your parents influence or control your decisions?

When asked "How do I deal with substance abuse?" two modern Jewish commentators gave this answer:

The first thing to do is accept the fact that life is sometimes harsh. Few things in life come easy, especially those things which we value. Expect to be challenged; expect to meet frustration. Then work as hard as you can to overcome the obstacles before you and revel in your achievement.

Among the obstacles you will face will be the temptation to do drugs. Practice saying "no" and feeling OK about going against the tide. Taking drugs (including alcohol) may feel good, but it doesn't help you achieve the goals you value. Instead of getting involved with drugs, get involved with people. Join a club, a study group, a sports team. Become more active in your youth group. Do volunteer work. Helping others is one of the best ways you can help yourself to feel worthwhile. Then drugs won't matter.

In this Dutch rehabilitation center, drug addicts seek to break their habit and start a new life.

Do parents have the right to commit a drug-abusing child to a treatment center even if the child doesn't want to go?

That leads to our last suggestion. If you want to feel better about yourself (and who doesn't?), set reasonably high standards for yourself, and try meeting them. Structure your life so that even you would be proud of you!

Ellen Goldsmith and Howard Laibson, in Keeping Posted, vol. 31, no. 6, p. 5

Do you find this advice convincing? What effect do you think it would have on someone your age who is already addicted to either alcohol or drugs?

What would you do if you found out your best friend was:

- Experimenting with marijuana?

- Using marijuana regularly?

- Using other drugs?

- Dealing drugs?

- Stealing to support a drug habit?

What would you say to your friend? What would you do if your direct efforts failed? Under what conditions would you tell what you knew to other friends? To your friend's parents? To school officials? To the police?

CHAPTER FOUR

SLOW! DANGER AHEAD!

Are you unhappy with yourself? Do you tend to exaggerate your weaknesses and minimize your strengths? Or are you able to accept yourself as you are?

Eating disorders

Rabbi Akiba said, "A man is not permitted to harm himself."
Mishnah Baba Kamma 90a

In Chapter Three we examined alcohol, tobacco, and drugs—substances through which people seek immediate pleasure at the price of eventual suffering. In this chapter, we will examine other kinds of self-destructive behavior, including the ultimate form of self-destruction, suicide.

One type of substance abuse to which people your age are especially vulnerable involves food—plain, ordinary, wholesome food. It's normal to experience variations in appetite, to eat more after exercising vigorously and during a growth spurt, to eat less after being relatively inactive. But the victims (usually girls) of a disorder known as *anorexia* eat so little that they literally starve themselves, sometimes to the point of emaciation or death. The opposite extreme is *bulimia*, in which the afflicted indulge in continual binges, stuffing themselves with excessive amounts of food. In a combined form of eating disorder, sometimes called *bulimarexia* or *bulimia nervosa*, the bulimic binges and then purges herself with laxatives or self-induced vomiting, in order to avoid gaining weight.

A victim of anorexia nervosa. Doctors have inserted a feeding tube through her nose.

Some people take their own lives with one swift stroke, while others destroy themselves more slowly. What kinds of behavior might be considered slow suicide?

Thin fox, fat fox

The Bible says, "As he came out of his mother's womb, so must he depart at last, naked as he came" (Ecclesiastes 5:14).

This might be compared to a fox who found a vineyard that was closed on all sides, except for one small hole in it. He tried to enter, but could not.

What did he do? He fasted for three days until he became thin and scrawny. Then he entered through the hole. He ate from the vineyard, becoming sleek and fat. When he wanted to leave, he could not get through the hole. So he fasted for three days until he became thin and scrawny again. Then he went out.

On leaving, he looked at the vineyard and said, "O vineyard, how beautiful you are and how good your fruit is! But what enjoyment have you given me? In the state in which one enters, one must leave."

Ecclesiastes Rabbah 5:14

If we interpret this parable as a commentary on Ecclesiastes 5:14, what does the vineyard represent? What is the "state in which one enters"? What is the state in which "one must leave"? Which eating disorder does the fox's behavior most closely resemble: anorexia, bulimia, or bulimarexia? Does the fox derive any benefit from the food it consumes? When the fox leaves the vineyard, is it better or worse off than when it entered?

You're not anorexic just because you diet for a week to lose a pound or two. You're not bulimic just because you eat a second scoop of ice cream at lunch. Both anorexia and bulimia are severe psychological disorders with serious health implications. Anorexics will not or cannot eat; bulimics will not or cannot stop eating; bulimarexics will not or cannot stop binging and purging.

What causes these eating disorders?

Sometimes a girl becomes obsessed with the idea that thin women are sexually attractive; movies, television, and magazines all reinforce this impression. She eats less and less until—in the words of one expert on anorexia—she becomes "addicted to starvation." Anorexia is a well-known medical problem in such fields as fashion modeling and ballet, where extreme thinness may be a professional requirement.

More often, eating disorders have subconscious motivations. Food is more than the calories we consume to keep our bodies going; it is also one of our earliest and most powerful symbols of love. Mothers show how much they love their babies by feeding them. Babies respond by eating and gaining weight. Far beneath the level of consciousness, the anorexic may be rebelling against her parents, the bulimic still desperately seeking her mother's approval. Or both may be fleeing from their emerging sexuality, the anorexic by coming to resemble a man more than a woman, the bulimic by making herself grossly unattractive.

Caring for your body

Judaism recognizes the importance of showing respect for the body through proper cleanliness, nutrition, exercise, and rest.

Once when Hillel had finished teaching his students, he walked toward home with them. "Master," they asked, "where are you going?"

"To perform a religious duty," he answered.

"What duty is it?"

"To bathe in the bathhouse."

They asked in surprise, "Is that a religious duty?"

He replied: "If someone is appointed to scrape and clean the statues of the king that stand in the theaters and circuses, is paid for the work and even associates with the nobility, how much more should I, who am created in God's image, take care of my body!"

Leviticus Rabbah 34:3

How do you feel if you don't have time to take a shower or bath when you need one? If you don't have enough time to wash and dry your hair? Do you feel the same way about skipping a meal or eating only a candy bar and soda instead of a nutritious dinner? If not, why not? In general, does keeping clean enhance your sense of well-being? When do you feel better about yourself: when you eat mostly junk food or when you maintain a well-balanced diet?

Since by keeping the body in health and strength one walks in the ways of God . . . it is a person's duty to avoid whatever is harmful to the body and cultivate habits conducive to good health.

Maimonides, Code, "Laws Concerning Moral Dispositions and Ethical Conduct," 4:1

If they were alive today, what would Hillel and Maimonides say to the anorexic and the bulimic? To the drug abuser, the chain smoker, or the alcoholic? To you?

Why did the rabbis call taking good care of your body a religious duty?

Canadian sprinter Ben Johnson (third from left) sets a record pace in the 100-meter dash.

Faster, faster!

While eating disorders are far more common among females than males, a related problem that occurs far more frequently among males is the use of steroids to enhance athletic performance. Steroids are chemical compounds that can temporarily give an athlete an unfair competitive advantage but which can also have serious—even fatal—side effects when used over a sustained period of time.

You may remember that during the 1988 Summer Olympics, a Canadian sprinter, Ben Johnson, was stripped of his gold medal in the men's 100-meter dash when a routine test discovered the steroid stanozolol in his urine. At the time, a member of the International Olympic Committee said of him: "Ben Johnson has just been killed as an athlete, and probably his complete life has been ruined."

A subdued Johnson, stripped of his gold medal, heads home after the 1988 Summer Olympics.

What are the long-term health risks of steroid use? Are athletes who use steroids and other chemicals being fair to their competitors? To themselves?

Like the anorexic and bulimic, the steroid-abusing athlete isn't happy with what he is. Just as the anorexic and bulimic alter their food intake to become something they're not, so the steroid-abusing athlete alters his chemical balance to increase his muscle mass or become more aggressive. Like an anorexic driven to near-starvation in order to attain a body type society promotes as attractive, the steroid-abuser risks his life in pursuit of the huge social and financial rewards our society confers on athletic success.

Learning to accept yourself

Such forms of substance abuse are a particular danger to you in part because so many adolescents are at least temporarily dissatisfied with themselves. They often exaggerate their weaknesses while minimizing their strengths, focus on what's wrong but overlook what's right. You will be a happy, healthy, mature person when you can accept yourself as you are, weak in some ways, strong in others, always trying to improve without ever expecting to be perfect.

What makes you feel depressed? What helps you get over your feelings of depression? Do you have someone you can share your problems with?

Ben Zoma says, "Who is wise? He who learns from everyone. . . . Who is strong? He who controls his impulses. . . . Who is rich? He who is happy with his portion."

Pirke Avot 4:1

Before he died, Rabbi Zusya said, "In the world to come they will not ask me, 'Why were you not Moses?' They will ask me, 'Why were you not Zusya?'"

Rabbi Zusya of Hanipol

What do you think Zusya meant by his final question? What do you regard as your best qualities? Are you able to express them as frequently as you'd like? What can you do to develop them and express them more often?

Heading for self-destruction

Roger hasn't been able to sleep more than a few minutes at a time since Thursday, when he spent the evening with his best friend, Ed. Although Roger had noticed for some time that Ed seemed depressed, he was shocked beyond belief to hear Ed say he was contemplating suicide.

Since Ed's girlfriend had broken off their relationship, nothing had gone right for him. His grades at school had hit bottom. He couldn't concentrate on anything. There were endless arguments with his parents over just about everything. Even the foods he used to enjoy seemed now like tasteless mush in his mouth. His beer and wine drinking had increased, and the songs he listened to again and again were filled with images of death and violence.

Ed had pledged Roger to secrecy before telling him what he was thinking. The two of them had shared many confidences. Neither had ever broken the bond of secrecy. They trusted each other totally.

If you were Roger, what would you do now? Try to persuade Ed not to go through with it? Propose an outing—a movie, a concert—that will get Ed's mind off his troubles? Warn Ed's parents or rabbi or a teacher you both trust? Should you risk Ed's friendship by violating his confidence? Or should you keep the secret and risk the possibility that Ed may follow through on his threat?

What could you say to persuade someone not to commit suicide?

Keeping secrets

Telling others about a friend's suicidal plans or actions may mean making a painful decision to break a confidence. A boy may whisper that he has loaded his father's gun and plans to use it on himself. Or a girl may confide, as Laurie did to her friends, that she slashed her wrists and bandaged them, but her parents know nothing about the event. You swear to keep the secret. And you find yourself in the untenable position of feeling responsible for your friend, yet not knowing what to do to help. If you break the confidence and tell oth-ers, you will enrage your friend and probably lose the friendship. But if you keep the information to yourself and your friend attempts or completes suicide, you will feel guilty and responsible for years to come.

Keep this in mind. Your first responsibility in any suicidal situation is to preserve life, not friendship. The secret you have been asked to keep is not an ordinary one. And the confidence itself may have been a disguised message or plea for help.

F. Klagsbrun, Too Young to Die *(Pocket Books, 1985), p. 86*

Do you agree with the author of this passage? Which do you think is more important: respecting Ed's confidence or trying to prevent him from committing suicide? Suppose that after telling somebody what Ed told you, you found out that Ed's threat wasn't really serious. Would you still feel you had done the right thing?

Reckoning

Scripture says, "For your lifeblood too I will require a reckoning" (Genesis 9:5).

Rabbi Eleazar taught that this means, "I will require a reckoning from you for your own lifeblood."

Baba Kamma 91b

The following passage reflects a time when the Romans made the teaching of Torah punishable by death.

Rabbi Ḥananiah ben Teradyon was found by the Romans studying Torah, publicly holding gatherings of pupils. . . .

They wrapped him in the scroll, placed bundles of branches around him, and set them on fire. Then they brought tufts of wool that had been soaked in water and placed them near his heart so that he should not die quickly. . . .

His disciples called to him, "Rabbi, what do you see?"

He answered, "The parchment is burning, but the letters are soaring upward."

"Open your mouth so that the fire will penetrate you," they said.

He answered, "Let Him who gave me my soul take it away, but none should injure himself."

Avodah Zarah 18a

Why did Rabbi Ḥananiah refuse to open his mouth in order to die more quickly? Couldn't someone say he had already injured himself by publicly teaching Torah after the Romans made it a capital offense? How might Rabbi Ḥananiah have defended his actions?

For a suicide no [funeral] rites should be observed. . . . There may be no rending of clothes, no baring of shoulders, and no eulogizing for him. The general rule is: The public should participate in whatever is done out of respect for the living; it should not participate in whatever is done out of respect for the dead.

Jerusalem Talmud, Semaḥot 2:1-4

Why do you think the ancient rabbis believed a suicide victim was unworthy of respect? Do you agree?

Finding a balance

The previous selections suggest that Jewish tradition has been unmitigatedly opposed to suicide under all conditions. Closer investigation reveals, however, the same kind of balancing effort our authorities tried to achieve on other issues.

Having decreed that certain funeral rites are to be denied those who kill themselves, the rabbis then found it difficult to label any specific case as suicide.

Who is to be counted a suicide?

Not one who climbs to the top of a tree or to the top of a roof and falls to his death. Rather it is one who says, "Behold, I am going to climb to the top of the tree [or] to the top of the roof, and then throw myself down to my death," and thereupon others see him climb to the top of the tree or to the top of the roof and fall to his death. . . .

If a person is found strangled hanging from a tree, or slain impaled upon a sword, he is presumed to have taken his own life unwittingly; to such a person no [funeral] rites may be denied.

Ibid.

In general terms, what proof was needed in rabbinic times before someone could be labeled a suicide? If such proof was unavailable, how did the rabbis expect the victim to be treated? Suppose the day after Ed told Roger he was contemplating suicide, Ed was found dead in a car crash on a deserted country road. How willing might you be to label his death a suicide? Could his death have been called a suicide by rabbinic standards? If not, why not? What does this tell us about how much confidence the rabbis had in rumors, gossip, and assumptions about what might have happened?

The fortress of Masada, where 960 Jews committed suicide so the Romans could not capture and kill them.

Do you feel that the Jews who died at Masada were heroes? Can taking one's own life ever be justified?

Martyrs of Masada

We have seen that (a) Judaism strictly prohibits suicide yet (b) is reluctant to brand the death of any particular person a suicide unless the evidence is overwhelming and incontrovertible. Even in the presence of such evidence, however, there have been times in Jewish history when people who committed suicide were honored as heroes.

You have undoubtedly read or heard about Masada. Perhaps you have even visited the remains of that mountain fortress in Israel. In the year 73 C.E. about a thousand men, women, and children at Masada were the very last Jewish holdouts against Roman conquest. When it became apparent that further resistance would be futile, they drew lots to determine the order in which they would die. Then they committed mass suicide rather than wait to be slaughtered by the Romans. According to the Jewish historian Josephus, 960 persons thus ended their lives. Two women and five children survived to tell the story.

Compare the behavior of these Jews to that of Ḥananiah ben Teradyon, described on p. 37. If Ḥananiah had been at Masada, what do you think he would have advised?

Hero of the Resistance

Samuel Zygelbojm, a leader of the Jewish community in Poland during World War II, escaped to London, where he tried desperately but in vain to call the world's attention to the Nazis' murderous assault against the Jews of Europe. When the world refused to heed, he committed suicide on 12 May 1943, addressing the following words to "the Polish Government, the Polish people, the Allied Governments and their peoples, and the conscience of the world."

Let my death be an energetic cry of protest against the indifference of the world which witnesses the extermination of the Jewish people without taking any steps to prevent it. In our day and age, human life is of little value; having failed to achieve success in my life, I hope that my death may jolt the indifference of those who, perhaps even in this extreme moment, could save the Jews who are still alive in Poland.

F. Klagsbrun, Voices of Wisdom *(Pantheon, 1980), pp. 490f*

Do you feel Samuel Zygelbojm was justified in committing suicide? Or do you think he should have continued to dedicate his efforts to saving the Jews of Poland? What might Rabbi Ḥananiah have said about Zygelbojm's decision?

Too real

The story of Roger and Ed is fictional, but the facts that underlie it are all too true. The suicide rate in the United States among young people aged fifteen to twenty-four tripled between the 1950s and the 1980s. Many reckless drivers, drug abusers, chain smokers, alcoholics, anorexics, and bulimics may also be attempting—usually unconsciously rather than consciously—to end their lives.

The reasons for these acts of desperation vary greatly, but the most important common element is probably a sense of hopelessness brought on by the death of a loved one, the breakup of a relationship, a failure at school or in some other activity, friction at home, a sense of abandonment by a parent, or some similar source of anxiety or disappointment. The poten- tial suicide may first turn to alcohol and drugs to ease the pain, but these only deepen the sense of overwhelming, hopeless depression.

What young people especially need to recognize is that even the happiest life has its share of disappointments. Life is dynamic: the worst and apparently most hopeless of our troubles can be relieved if we do our best, a little each day, and give time a chance. One expert on youthful suicide puts it this way:

In Hebrew there is a word T'shuva. It means "to return," and implies the opportunity of a renewal attempt, a fresh start, an ever new beginning. Past failures need not doom a person forever. The willingness to build the temple of tomorrow's dreams on the grave of yesterday's bitterness is the greatest evidence of the unquenchable spirit that fires the soul of man.

Rabbi Earl Grollman, Suicide *(Beacon Press, 1971), p. 117.*

A college freshman who entered therapy after attempting suicide agrees:

"Now that I am well on my way to getting my head on straight finally, after all these years, I can honestly say that I feel that no matter what kind of bind you are in you should try your damnedest to get out of it, get yourself together, mentally and physically. Most people who have been using drugs or drinking and have become suicidal need therapy and someone to talk to. I myself see a social worker.

"No one can make you want to live. But believe me, life is too precious to throw away. I know. I would never be so foolish again. I'm just glad I faced up to myself. Now I *love* me."

Klagsbrun, Too Young To Die, *p. 150*

How you can help

Perhaps the following suggestions will help you if you or a friend of yours ever have to deal with a suicidal crisis.

Recognize the clues to suicide. Look for symptoms of deep depression and signs of hopelessness and helplessness. Listen for suicide threats and words of warning, such as "I wish I were dead," or "I have nothing to live for." Watch for despairing actions and signals of loneliness; notice whether the person becomes withdrawn and isolated from others. Be alert to suicidal thoughts as a depression lifts.

Trust your own judgment. If you believe someone is in danger of suicide, act on your beliefs. Don't let others mislead you into ignoring suicidal signals.

Tell others. As quickly as possible share your knowledge with parents, friends, teachers, or other people who might help in a suicidal crisis. Don't worry about breaking a confidence if someone reveals suicidal plans to you. You may have to betray a secret to save a life.

Stay with a suicidal person. Don't leave a suicidal person alone if you think there is immediate danger. Stay with the person until help arrives or a crisis passes.

Listen intelligently. Encourage a suicidal person to talk to you. Don't give false reassurances that "everything will be O.K." Listen and sympathize with what the person says.

Urge professional help. Put pressure on a suicidal person to seek help from a psychiatrist, psychologist, social worker, or other professional during a suicidal crisis or after a suicide attempt. Encourage the person to continue with therapy even when it becomes difficult.

Be supportive. Show the person that you care. Help the person feel worthwhile and wanted again.

Ibid., p. 96

How realistic are these ideas? Which one do you feel would be most helpful? Least helpful? From your own experience, do you feel that this list needs to be modified in any way? What additional suggestions would you make?

Breaking up a protest outside the Soviet consulate in
New York City.

**How much are you willing to risk in order to stand
up for your beliefs?**

CHAPTER FIVE

ARMY OR PRISON?

Pacifism and war

One of my closest colleagues and friends
is Rabbi Jerome Malino. Before World
War II, both of us were absolute pacifists
—that is, we were conscientious objec-
tors who had vowed never to participate
in war. Rabbi Malino and I were in complete agreement until after the United
States entered World War II. Sometime in
1942 my position changed; his did not.
After much painful inner struggle and
more than a few sleepless nights, I called
for a commission in the Navy and served
ultimately as Jewish chaplain in the Fifth
Marine Division that conquered Iwo Jima.
Why this drastic change?

In the first place, I concluded that a
Hitler victory would mean the absolute
destruction of the Jewish people. Of more
immediate practical concern was that
many thousands of young American Jews
(including several in my own congregation), lacking the choice I enjoyed as a
member of the clergy, were being drafted.
They would no doubt need support from
a rabbi more than ever before in their
lives. How could I let them down?

Rabbi Malino also felt the need to resist Nazism, but he explains that he remained a pacifist because he believed "that if the world were ever to outgrow the violent solution of international differences it would be because some hardy spirits never faltered in their commitment to peace." He served the needs of Jewish soldiers by accepting a civilian chaplaincy at a military convalescent center for the remainder of the war.

I continue to respect and admire Rabbi Malino; he is among my very close and cherished friends. He acted in accordance with his conscience, just as I did according to mine. Who do you think made the right decision? If you had been eligible to serve in World War II, would you have wanted to take up arms against Germany and Japan? If not, in what other ways might you have helped the war against Hitler?

The right not to fight

Both explicitly and by implication, Judaism has long recognized that some people need not serve in the armed forces.

Then the officials shall address the troops as follows, "Is there anyone who has built a new house but has not dedicated it? Let him go back to his home, lest he die in battle and another dedicate it. Is there anyone who has planted a vineyard but has never harvested it? Let him go back to his home, lest he die in battle and another initiate it. Is there anyone who has spoken for a woman in marriage, but who has not yet married her? Let him go back to his home, lest he die in battle and another marry her. . . . Is there anyone afraid and disheartened? Let him go back to his home, lest the courage of his comrades flag like his."**

Deuteronomy 20:5-8

Why are both terms "afraid" and "disheartened" used? To indicate that even the most physically powerful and courageous, if he is compassionate, should be exempted.

Rabbi Akiba, Tosafot to Sotah 8:6

According to Rabbi Akiba's commentary, who should be exempted from fighting? Why should this be so? Couldn't it be argued that if wars have to be fought, it's better that soldiers be compassionate rather than brutal?

The following do not move from their place [to join the army]: He who built a new house and dedicated it, planted a new vineyard and used its fruit, married his betrothed, or took home his brother's childless widow. . . . These do not even supply water and food or repair the roads [for the army].

Mishnah Sotah 8:4

Let a man ever be among the pursued, not among the pursuers.

Rabbi Abahu, Babba Kamma 93a

Explain in your own words what you think Rabbi Abahu meant by this statement. Do you agree? Do you think Abahu would have supported the right of people to defend themselves if attacked? To retaliate against their attackers? To strike the first blow when threatened with attack?

Conscientious objection to military service is in accordance with the highest interpretation of Judaism.

Central Conference of American Rabbis (Reform)

We recognize the right of the conscientious objector to claim exemption from military service in any war in which he cannot give his moral assent, and we pledge ourselves to support him in his determination to refrain from any participation in it.

Rabbinical Assembly of America (Conservative)

Peace

In addition to defending the right of some people not to fight, Judaism places extraordinary emphasis on peace as the noblest of all ethical values.

David said to Solomon, "My son, as for me, it was in my heart to build a house unto the name of the Lord my God. But the word of the Lord came to me, saying, 'You have shed blood abundantly and have made great wars; you shall not build a house unto My name, because you have shed much blood upon the earth. . . .'"

I Chronicles 22:7-8

Joshua leads the Israelites in the battle of Jericho.

How do you reconcile Judaism's commitment to peace with the fact that so many Jewish heroes have been military leaders?

Be of the disciples of Aaron, seek peace and pursue it!

Pirke Avot 1:12

The law does not order you to run after or pursue the other commandments, but only to fulfill them on the appropriate occasion. But peace you must seek in your own place and pursue it even to another place as well.

Midrash to Pirke Avot 1:12

Great is peace, for the prophets have taught all people to care for nothing so much as peace. . . .

Great is peace, for it outweighs everything. We say in the morning prayers: "He makes peace and creates everything." Without peace there is nothing. . . .

Great is peace, for the Holy One created no finer attribute than peace.

Midrash to Numbers Rabbah 11:7

If Jewish tradition values peace so highly, why has the history of Israel —both ancient and modern—been one of almost incessant warfare? How do you reconcile Judaism's emphasis on peace with the fact that some of our greatest heroes—David, Joshua, Deborah, Judah Maccabee —were leaders in battle?

Supporters of Rabbi Meir Kahane demand that "not one inch" of the captured territories be surrendered.

"Peace Now" demonstrators call on the Israeli government to withdraw from territories captured during the 1967 war.

Do you believe Israel should be willing to give up all or some of the captured territories in order to make peace with the Arabs? What concessions, if any, should the Israeli government demand before agreeing to negotiate with the Palestine Liberation Organization?

Do you feel modern Israel has done all it can to make peace with its Arab neighbors? Do you feel Israel's Arab neighbors have done all they can to make peace with the Jewish state? What do you think is the best way to achieve lasting peace in the Middle East? What role, if any, should the United States and the Soviet Union have in bringing peace between Arabs and Israel? What role, if any, might Israel and the Jewish people play in fostering peace between the United States and the Soviet Union?

Ground rules

Wars generally were divided by Jewish tradition into two broad categories. Every Jew had to fight in a *milkhemet ḥovah* or *milkhemet mitzvah*, an obligatory war or one waged in pursuit of a *mitzvah*. These were wars on which the survival of Judaism or the Jewish people depended. Such a war could be declared unilaterally by the king.

Each individual Jew could decide on the basis of his own conscience and judgment, however, whether to fight in a *milkhemet r'shut*, a voluntary or permissive war. Any conflict undertaken for territorial expansion or to secure economic or political advantage was in this category. A *milkhemet r'shut* could be declared only by vote of the Sanhedrin, representing the people who would actually have to fight.

Define in your own words the terms *milkhemet mitzvah* and *milkhemet r'shut*. Into which category would you place each of the following wars? If you're not sure, consult your school or temple library. Be prepared to support your opinion.

- World War I
- World War II
- The Vietnam war
- US support for the contras in Nicaragua
- Israel's wars with Arab nations in (a) 1948, (b) 1956, (c) 1973
- Israel's 1982 war in Lebanon
- Israel's suppression, beginning in late 1987, of Arab uprisings on the West Bank, in Gaza, and elsewhere.

Was the Vietnam war a *milkhemet mitzvah* or a *milkhemet r'shut*? If you had been called up for the draft during the time when U.S. troops were fighting in Vietnam, would you have agreed to serve? Registered as a conscientious objector? Searched for other legal ways to avoid wartime service? Fled to Canada? Burned your draft card and gone to jail?

Specific limitations

In addition to distinguishing between obligatory and voluntary wars, Jewish tradition placed more specific limitations on how wars could be fought.

1. The safety of neutrals and civilians must be preserved.

When it takes up arms, [the Jewish nation] distinguishes between those whose life is one of hostility, and the reverse. For to breathe slaughter against all, even those who have done very little or nothing amiss, shows what I would call a savage and brutal soul.

Josephus, The Special Laws *4:224f*

2. A city may not be placed under siege unless first offered peace terms.

When you approach a town to attack it, you shall offer it terms of peace. . . . If it does not surrender to you, but would join battle with you, you shall lay siege to it.

Deuteronomy 20:10-12

God commanded Moses to make war on Sichon . . . but he did not do so. Instead, he sent messengers . . . to Sichon . . . with an offer of peace (Deuteronomy 2:26). God said to him: "I commanded you to make war with him, but instead you began with peace; by your life, I shall confirm your decision. Every war upon which Israel enters shall begin with an offer of peace."

Deuteronomy Rabbah 5:13

3. Even after a city has been put under siege, an escape route must be left open for its inhabitants.

When siege is laid to a city for the purpose of capture, it may not be surrounded on all four sides, but only on three in order to give an opportunity for escape to those who would flee to save their lives.

Maimonides, Mishneh Torah 7:7

4. The ecosystem must be preserved, in order to ensure human survival after the conflict has ended.

When in your war against a city you have to besiege it a long time in order to capture it, you must not destroy its trees, wielding the ax against them. You may eat of them, but you must not cut them down. Are trees of the field human to withdraw before you under siege? Only trees which you know do not yield food may be destroyed.

Deuteronomy 20:19-20

Today we recognize that trees play an important ecological role beyond the food they produce. Do you think the rule forbidding destruction only of fruit trees needs to be broadened? How might observance of such a broader rule make besieging a city more difficult?

5. Excessive or unnecessary damage to property must be avoided.

Also, one who smashes household goods, tears clothes, demolishes a building, stops up a spring, or destroys articles of food with destructive intent, transgresses the command, "You shall not destroy."

Maimonides, Mishneh Torah, Hilkhot M'lakhim *6:10*

In modern times, nations have tried to place additional limitations on warfare —for example, by banning the use of chemical and biological weapons. How successful have these limitations been?

Do you believe there should also be a ban on the use of nuclear weapons? Should nations continue to develop and stockpile devices whose use in wartime has been outlawed?

In general, do you support such attempts to limit specific weapons and tactics? Or do you believe, as the saying goes, that "all's fair in love and war"?

Registering for the draft

Some of you will need to make a very specific peace-related decision within the next several years.

David will graduate from high school in June, three months from now, and will turn eighteen in August. At that time, according to a law enacted in 1980, he will be required to register for a possible future military draft.

Since all that's involved right now is signing on the proper line, why is this such a problem for him? Mainly because he is enrolled in a peace study group and considers himself, like Rabbi Malino, to be a conscientious objector to all war. He considers any kind of cooperation with the Pentagon sinful, and the thought of registering for a future draft turns his stomach. Yet the consequences of disobeying the law are unpleasant.

Israeli soldiers on patrol in Jerusalem.

Israel and its Arab neighbors have been at war for more than forty years. How has this prolonged war affected the State of Israel? Its Jewish majority? Its Arab minority? The Palestinians who live in Israeli-occupied territories? The United States? The attitude of American Jews toward the Jewish state?

Andy Mager and Sheila Parks know that. Because Andy refused to register for the draft in 1985, he was sentenced to six months in federal prison plus two and one-half years of probation. Sheila's antiwar protest went even farther than Andy's. She is one of five persons who broke into the General Dynamics Electric Boat shipyard at Quonset Point, R.I., where they hammered three Trident II missile tubes into the shapes of plowshares and pruning hooks. This was in literal fulfillment of Isaiah's prophecy:

And they shall beat their swords into plowshares and their spears into pruning hooks. Nation shall not lift up sword against nation, neither shall they learn war any more.

Isaiah 2:4

Sheila and her companions were sentenced to three years in prison, with an additional suspended sentence of two years.

Every ethical decision has costs and consequences. The prophet Amos was banished from the northern kingdom of Israel and sent back to his native Judah. Jeremiah was arrested and thrown into a pit. Andy Mager and Sheila Parks aren't the only young Jews today who know the cost of ethical choices. David cannot afford to be naive.

Do you think Andy Mager and Sheila Parks were right in what they did? Do you believe prison is an appropriate punishment for those who break the law out of deep moral or religious conviction? If not, what other form of service might be more appropriate?

Female munitions workers during World War I.

Must people who support the cause of peace refuse to work in weapons factories? Boycott companies that make bombs?

In your opinion, which of the activities listed below can contribute most to the attainment of peace? Which will contribute least? Why? What are the advantages and disadvantages of each? Which, if any, are you prepared to undertake now?

■ Support candidates and programs that promise to preserve peace and deter aggression by increasing the nation's military strength.

■ Campaign for peace and antiwar candidates and for reductions in the defense budget.

■ Become active in major organizations working for peace and international understanding.

■ Refuse to work in a plant that makes weapons systems or components for the military.

■ March in protest at draft registration offices trying to persuade people not to sign up.

■ Refuse to register for a possible military draft.

■ Break into a weapons plant, as Sheila Parks did, to destroy the components being manufactured there.

Disobeying

David's dilemma and the examples of Andy Mager and Sheila Parks raise the broader question of whether people ever have the moral right to disobey the law. This problem is especially acute in a democracy, where the laws are made by the people and their elected representatives.

Martin Luther King, Jr., argued that sometimes we have not only the right but the obligation to disobey an unjust law. In 1963, King was imprisoned for violating an Alabama segregation law. From his Birmingham jail cell he wrote a letter to eight white clergymen who had publicly protested his activities. In the letter, scribbled on scraps of newspaper and toilet tissue, he said:

One may well ask, "How can you advocate breaking some laws and obeying others?" The answer lies in the fact that there are two types of laws, just and unjust. One has not only a legal but a moral responsibility to obey just laws. One has a moral responsibility to disobey unjust laws. . . . Any law that uplifts human personality is just, any law that degrades human personality is unjust. . . . An individual who breaks a law that conscience tells him is unjust, and willingly accepts the penalty of imprisonment in order to arouse the conscience of the community over its injustice, is in reality expressing the highest respect for law.

Do you agree with Dr. King's distinction between just and unjust laws? With his conditions that justify disobedience of the law? Does the draft registration law bothering David uplift or degrade human personality? Why?

Protesters marching from Selma to Montgomery, Ala., in 1965 brave police brutality and Ku Klux Klan violence.

A demonstration in New York City sponsored by the Congress of Racial Equality.

Do people have the moral obligation to disobey an unjust law?

Respect for law

Jewish tradition supports both respect for law and the right, under certain conditions, to disobey it.

Pray for the welfare of the government, for were it not for the fear it inspires, every man would swallow his neighbor alive.

Pirke Avot 3:2

Scripture says: "You have made [humanity] like the fish of the sea . . . " (Habakkuk 1:14).

Why are people compared to the fish of the sea?

Just as among the fish of the sea the larger ones swallow the smaller ones, so it is with people. If it were not for the fear of government, the stronger would swallow the weaker.

Avodah Zarah 4a

Do you agree with the idea that the true purpose of law is to prevent the strong from victimizing the weak? Might this idea help us decide whether a particular law is just or unjust? Using this principle, give an example of a just law and an unjust law.

The next three passages, in condoning disobedience to certain decrees, offer a different way of distinguishing just from unjust laws.

The king of Egypt spoke to the Hebrew midwives . . . saying, "When you deliver the Hebrew women . . . if it is a boy, kill him; if it is a girl, let her live." The midwives, fearing God, did not do as the king of Egypt had told them; they let the boys live.

Exodus 1:15-17

The Boston Tea Party (1773).

Were the colonists right to destroy other people's property in order to protest a law they believed was unfair?

And [King Saul] commanded the guards standing by, "Turn about and kill the priests of the Lord, for they are in league with David; they knew he was running away and they did not inform me." But the king's servants would not raise a hand to strike down the priests of the Lord.

I Samuel 22:17

Whoever disregards a royal order because he is busy with God's commandments—even the slightest commandment—is exempt [from blame or punishment]. If the master's orders conflict with the servant's, the master's take precedence. And it goes without saying that if a king ordered a violation of God's commandments, he is not to be obeyed.

Maimonides, Code, Hilkhot M'lakhim 3:9

How does Maimonides distinguish between laws that should be obeyed and laws that shouldn't? Does this mean that anyone can justify committing any crime just by saying, "God told me to do it"? Today we live in a pluralistic society in which people of different religions hold different beliefs about what God commands them to do. Does this weaken or strengthen our ability to use religious arguments to challenge a law we consider unjust?

CHAPTER SIX

"WHO IS WISE ENOUGH...?"

Death—the ultimate injustice?

Job's question

Have you ever experienced the death of someone you loved very much? A grandparent or parent? A brother or sister? A cherished friend?

How did you feel? What questions did you ask? What rituals, if any, did you perform in your quest for solace and understanding? Did they help?

There has probably never been a person more devastatingly crushed by the death of loved ones than Job. Are you familiar with his story, recounted in the biblical book that bears his name? On a single day all his property was destroyed and every one of his sons and daughters was killed. His closest friends tried in vain to comfort him. His wife's advice was ''Blaspheme God and die!'' But Job persisted in protesting his innocence and demanding to know why he was made to suffer. Finally, he heard a voice, addressing him out of a tempest:

**Who is this who darkens counsel,
Speaking without knowledge?
Gird your loins like a man;
I will ask and you will inform Me.
Where were you when I laid the earth's foundations?
Speak if you have understanding. . . .
Who is wise enough to give an account of the heavens?**

Job 38:1-4, 37

If you were Job, would you curse your fate, as Job's wife urged him, or demand to know the reason for your suffering?

Assuming that God is the source of these words, what is He really telling Job? Has He eased Job's anguish? If you were Job, would these words give you any real comfort?

The ultimate injustice?

A friend of mine describes death as "the ultimate injustice." Do you agree with him? Is death always unjust? Sometimes? Never?

"And God saw all that He had made, and behold it was very good" (Genesis 1:31).

Rabbi Meir said: " 'Behold it was very good' —this refers to death."

Genesis Rabbah 9:5

According to the commentator in Genesis Rabbah, why does the book of Genesis say "behold it was very good"? What does this imply about the role of death in God's creation? About the relationship between death and life?

The exact circumstances surrounding the death of the poet Ibn Gabirol are unknown. According to one legend, however, a certain Mohammedan, jealous of Ibn Gabirol's genius, killed him and buried his body beneath a tree. Some time after, people began to notice that a fig tree in the garden of the Mohammedan was bearing a particularly large and luscious fruit, like none that grew elsewhere. Curiosity was aroused, and the tree was dug up in order to discover the secret of its remarkable fertility. Then it was discovered that Ibn Gabirol was buried there.

Rabbi Jacob P. Rudin in S. Greenberg (ed.), Treasury of Comfort (Crown, 1954), p. 28

The parable about Solomon Ibn Gabirol conveys a powerful message concerning the legacy that great people leave us. Did the murder of Ibn Gabirol really eradicate his genius? How do you interpret the meaning of the ''large and luscious fruit'' that grew on the fig tree over his grave?

When Rabbi Bun died, Rabbi Zeiga eulogized as follows: "To what is the case of Rabbi Bun like? To a king who has hired workers for his garden, and he observes that one of them works expertly and efficiently. He calls the worker over and talks with him about the garden. In the evening, when the king pays all the gardeners, he gives the capable worker the same pay as the others. The others protest to the king: 'But he worked only two hours, and we worked eight.' 'True,' answers the king, 'but he accomplished more in two hours than you did in eight.' Rabbi Bun has labored in the Torah during his twenty-eight years more than another fine student in a hundred years."

Midrash adapted from ibid., *p. 158*

Who does ''the king'' stand for in the parable about Rabbi Bun? What does the pay the workers receive at the end of the day represent? How much comfort do you think this parable gave those mourning Rabbi Bun's death at the age of only twenty-eight?

A world without death

Have you ever wondered whether life would be happier in a world where no one ever died and nothing ever faded?

Simon mourned excessively for his departed friend. He was inconsolable in his grief. One night in a vision he heard a voice say to him reprovingly, "Why do you grieve so much? Is not death an inevitable incident in the cycle of life? Would you change the plan of the universe and make people immortal?"

Simon gathered his courage and he talked back: "Why not, O Lord?" . . .

And the voice replied, "So you deny the service of death to the economy of life?

Very well, then. We shall set you in a world where immortality prevails and see how you like it."

Simon looked at the countryside and understood the meaning of his dream. All this magnificence will endure forever. Nothing of it will perish. And so it indeed turned out to be.

Not a flower died on its stalk. Not a blossom fell from the lilac bushes. Summer gave way and autumn came, but not a leaf withered, not a tree lost its foliage. The world in all its beauty had

The funeral of President John F. Kennedy, assassinated on November 22, 1963.

Most people over forty can tell you exactly where they were and what they were doing when they first heard that Kennedy was shot. How did your parents and grandparents react to the news? How did they express their shock and grief?

been given a kind of fixed permanence, and it shone in the self-same lustre. At last life seemed to be freed from the ravages of time and circumstance.

But gradually Simon felt palled. Nothing died in his world, but nothing was born in it either. He was spared the ravages of age, but he missed seeing the wondrous dance of youth. His eyes tired at the beauty of flowers forever the same in hue. He longed to witness the glory of a new flower's unfolding. He was ready to renounce the gift of immortality when he suddenly awoke from his dream.

He brooded for a while over his strange experience and then he said: "O Lord, I thank You that You have made me a mortal of flesh and blood. Someone died that I might be born and I am willing to die that there may be growth and the emergence of new life. . . ."

Rabbi Ben Zion Bokser in ibid., *p. 185*

Stages of grief

For all of us, the loss of a loved one is one of life's most difficult burdens. At least for a while we may—consciously or unconsciously—deny that our loved one has really died. We may act as though he or she has left us just temporarily and will return soon. I once had a congregant who, for more than a year, kept all his deceased son's suits hanging exactly as they had been in the young man's closet.

As illusion gives way to reality, denial may be replaced by anger. We may focus our anger in any of several directions: at the person who has died, for leaving us so lonely; at the physician, who failed to prevent the death; at a living member of the family who, we feel, didn't do enough for the deceased; even at our rabbi, who offers such glib comfort and doesn't seem to realize just how much we have lost or how acute our pain is.

Feelings of guilt may follow. An eleven-year-old girl named Carla whose father died when she was eight expressed it this way:

I remember thinking that maybe his dying was some kind of punishment. I broke his typewriter in the office one time, and another time I broke his swivel chair and I thought it was as if I'd done all this bad stuff so, you know, his dying was like a punishment.

I don't think this anymore. I know he was really, really, really sick and that there was nothing that could really help him.

Jill Krementz (ed.), How It Feels When a Parent Dies *(Knopf, 1981), p. 78*

Shock, horror, disbelief, anger—Americans experienced all these emotions and more after the space shuttle Challenger exploded on January 28, 1986. Do you remember where you were and what you felt?

All these stages are normal as we recover from the death of someone we love. They become pathological only if we are unable gradually to grow through them and fail to resume a healthy, productive life.

A parent's death

Children who have lost a parent face an especially difficult problem when the surviving parent contemplates remarriage. Carla confronted this anxiety, too:

My mother has been seeing a man named John. He's divorced and his two children live with him. I hope they don't get married. . . . I don't want them to get married . . . because I know I would get mad at John for trying to replace my father. This year he took us down to Disney World and in a way it was fun, but in a way I felt sort of like my father would be mad at me because he always talked about taking us to Disney World and we always looked forward to that. So when we went with John, I felt that my father should be there. I didn't want my father to be mad at me for having a good time without him. I'm glad I went, but it made me feel very confused and it was sort of scary to me.

[Another] reason I don't want them to get married is because he has children and I know I'll have to share my mother with them. And since my father died, Jackie and I have gotten used to having her all to ourselves. Sometimes when she goes out with other people I just feel those people are trying to take her away from me.

Ibid., p. 81

Here again, Carla's fears were perfectly normal. It was healthy that she could express herself honestly and could slowly grow to accept and love John without feeling that she was betraying her father. With compassion and understanding on all sides, most children are able to accept and enjoy their new family relationships.

If one of your parents (or another close relative or friend) has died, did you experience any of the emotions described by Carla? Did you at first try to deny reality, to act as if you expected the dead parent to return? Did you feel hostility toward anyone? Guilt? With whom were you able to discuss your feelings freely? With whom do you wish you could have discussed them?

If you have a friend who has experienced the death of a loved one, try discussing these feelings with your friend.

Autopsy

A death in the family poses problems even before we can fully accept the reality of what has happened to us. Often, for example, the attending physician asks for permission surgically to examine the body. In the following selection, an eighteenth-century rabbi gives his response to the question of whether an autopsy may be performed in order to improve surgical techniques for the future:

The principle that even a possibility of saving a life waives . . . biblical commandments . . . applies only when there is before us concretely such a possibility, as for instance a person sick with that same ailment. In our case, however, there is no patient at hand whose treatment calls for this knowledge. It is only that people want to learn this skill for the future possibility that a patient who will need this treatment might come before us. For such a slight apprehension we do not nullify a biblical commandment or even a rabbinic prohibition.

Ezekiel ben Judah Landau of Prague, Responsa, Noda bi-Yehudah, Tinyana. Yoreh De'ah 210

[A]n autopsy would be warranted in order to secure information useful in treating another patient afflicted by the same disease, but not simply for the purpose of advancement of scientific knowledge even though new information gained as a result of the autopsy might, at some future time, contribute to the cure of gravely ill patients.

Rabbi J. David Bleich, Contemporary Halakhic Problems (Ktav/Yeshiva University Press, 1963), 2:57

In these days of speedy communication, patients are "at hand" everywhere awaiting the findings of anatomical research, and what is discovered in one place today may save a life in another place tomorrow.

The need for autopsies to conquer some of the worst scourges, such as cancer and heart disease, is, according to medical opinion, incontestable. . . .

The anticipated benefits from autopsies now include not only the hope of finding cures for obscure diseases but . . . testing the safety of the constant output of new drugs. . . .

Just as it is the duty of Rabbis to urge relatives not to consent to autopsies where life-saving considerations do not apply. . . they are religiously bound to advocate and encourage autopsies in cases where human lives may therefore be saved, in the same way that the suspension of the Sabbath laws in the face of danger to life is not merely optional but mandatory.

Immanuel Jakobovits, Jewish Medical Ethics (Bloch, 1975), pp. 282f

Why was Jewish tradition so restrictive in its attitude toward autopsy? Are there valid reasons for us to be less restrictive today? Does an autopsy indicate diminished respect for the sanctity of human life? It may interest you to know that all three of the rabbis quoted on this topic are Orthodox. What does their disagreement teach us about Judaism?

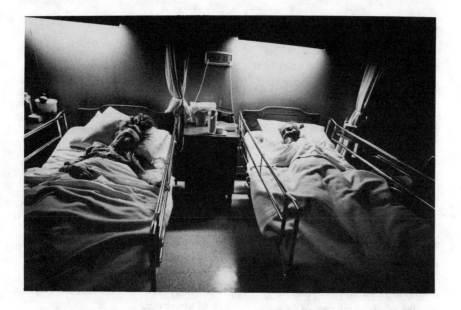

Burial

Another immediate problem when a family member dies is selecting a coffin. I have sometimes heard funeral directors suggest to mourners than an elaborate, expensive coffin shows how much they really loved the deceased. I have also heard survivors insist that money should not be "wasted" on a coffin but should instead be used to help the living—for example, to support heart or cancer research. What do you think? What does the following quotation from the Talmud tell us about how Jewish tradition views this question?

Formerly they used to bring out the deceased for burial, the rich on a tall bed, ornamented with rich covers, the poor on a plain box; and the poor felt ashamed. Therefore, a law was passed that all should be brought out on a plain box, in deference to the poor. . . .

Formerly the expense of burying the dead was harder for a family to bear than the death itself, so that sometimes family members fled to escape the expense. This was so until Rabban Gamaliel ordered that he be buried in a plain linen shroud instead of expensive garments.

Mo'ed Katan 27a-b

Which is more difficult for mourners to accept: the death of an elderly person, following prolonged illness, or a death that comes quickly and suddenly in a catastrophic accident?

Shivah and shloshim

Judaism has developed a system of rituals to guide us after a loved one dies. The seven days following a funeral are called *shivah*. Depending on how the Hebrew word is spelled, *shivah* can mean either "sitting" or "seven." During these seven days, tradition recommends that both morning and evening religious services be conducted in the home, that mourners sit on low stools or boxes, that no leather shoes be worn, and that all mirrors be covered. In addition, men do not shave, and women refrain from using cosmetics. A candle or lamp is kept burning throughout the week in memory of the deceased.

What is the purpose of such behavior? Which practices are aimed at showing respect for the deceased and which at comforting the mourners? If you have sat shivah yourself or have visited a Jewish house of mourning, which of these rituals have you found helpful and which not?

People sometimes feel awkward when visiting friends during shivah, not knowing whether to talk about the deceased, to make idle conversation, to act as if this were an ordinary social call, or just to remain silent. Apparently this was also a problem in ancient times.

How should a visitor behave in a house of mourning? According to the rabbis, a visitor should sit in silence (Berakhot 6b, Mo'ed Katan 28b). The ancient sages apparently felt that a mourner engrossed in his grief is in no mood for conversation. . . .

The maintenance of silence by visitors was an acceptable practice in ancient times because all mourners understood the significance of the silence. Modern people, not familiar with this practice, might misinterpret such silence as a sign of indifference. Visitors therefore feel constrained to express some sentiments that will ease the pain of the mourners. Unfortunately, the wisdom for choosing the right words at such a delicate moment eludes many people.

Rabbi A. P. Bloch, A Book of Jewish Ethical Concepts *(Ktav, 1984), pp. 234f*

Do you agree or disagree with Rabbi Bloch? Why? Is it more comforting for mourners to talk about the deceased, to express their feelings openly, perhaps to cry, or to be diverted to other topics of conversation? Would your answer be the same in all cases? Why?

The days following *shivah*, extending until thirty days after the funeral, are called *shloshim*, meaning "thirty." This is still a time of mourning, though less stringent than *shivah*. Mourners are no longer restricted to their homes, but they are still expected to refrain from any public entertainment or celebration.

Kaddish

From the conclusion of *shivah* until a year after the death, mourners are expected to recite the Kaddish prayer in the synagogue daily. Thereafter, they must recite Kaddish on the *yahrzeit* (anniversary) of the death.

Perhaps the most amazing aspect of the Kaddish prayer is that, although regularly recited in memory of the dead, it contains not a single word about death or dying:

Hallowed and enhanced may He be throughout the world of His own creation. May He cause His sovereignty soon to be accepted, during our life and the life of all Israel. And let us say: Amen.

May He be praised throughout all time.

Glorified and celebrated, lauded and praised, acclaimed and honored, extolled and exalted may the Holy One be, far beyond all song and psalm, beyond all tributes which can be uttered. And let us say: Amen.

Let there be abundant peace from Heaven, with life's goodness for us and for all the people Israel. And let us say: Amen.

May He who brings peace to His universe bring peace to us and to all the people Israel. And let us say: Amen.

Adapted from J. Harlow (ed.), Mahzor for Rosh Hashanah and Yom Kippur *(Rabbinical Assembly, 1972)*

Why should we thank God at a time of mourning? What themes in the Kaddish are also found in the words of the voice that spoke to Job from the tempest? To what kind of "peace" does the Kaddish refer? What significance does this prayer assign to the life of an individual? To the welfare of the Jewish people?

In Orthodox and most Conservative congregations, only mourners rise when the Kaddish is recited; in most Reform congregations, everyone rises. Which practice do you favor? Why? What are the advantages and disadvantages of each?

Rituals of memory

Jewish tradition and custom offer other ways for us to commemorate our departed loved ones. On Yom Kippur as well as on the closing days of Sukkot, Pesah, and Shavuot, a special memorial service (Yizkor) is held in the synagogue.

Some families visit the cemetery regularly, especially in anticipation of the High Holy Days. Tradition forbids such visits immediately after the funeral, at least until the end of *shloshim*. Can you think of a good reason for this prohibition?

The traditional funeral ceremony of walking seven times
around the body of the
deceased.

A Jewish cemetery.

**How much help and com-
fort do these mourning
practices provide?**

A synagogue memorial tablet, illuminated on each
yahrzeit.

Many congregations display memorial tablets with the name of the deceased illuminated in observance of his or her *yahrzeit*. Sometimes a family of wealth will contribute enough money to a college, a hospital, a temple, or some other public institution to have a building or part of one named after someone who has died.

How much comfort do you think each of these practices can bring to the mourners? Are there other ways in which the memory of a loved one can be perpetuated?

Balance

Our ancestors tried to strike a wholesome balance in their mourning practices. They realized that neither outright denial nor excessive and morbid preoccupation with death is healthy. We today—with our greater knowledge of psychology—are also aware of the fact that exaggerated mourning may mask inner feelings of hostility or guilt. Moderation marks the most genuine grief, without need for psychological camouflage.

A person who meets a mourner after a year and speaks words of consolation to him then, to what can he be compared?

To a physician who meets a person whose leg had been broken and healed, and says to him, "Let me break your leg again, and reset it, to convince you that my treatment was good."

Mo'ed Katan 21b

Mourn for a few days, as propriety demands, and then take comfort for your grief.

For grief may lead to death, and a sorrowful heart saps the strength. . . .

When the dead is at rest, let his memory rest too; take comfort as soon as he has breathed his last.

Wisdom of Ben Sira 38

If a funeral procession and a bridal procession meet each other on the way, the funeral procession should make way for the bridal procession. Likewise, if there are not enough people in the city to attend both, they bring the bride under the canopy first and then they bury the dead. . . .

In the case of a corpse and a circumcision, circumcision comes first.

Shulḥan Arukh, "Death and Mourning," chap. 380

Why should a bridal procession come before a funeral procession, and a circumcision take precedence over a corpse? What does this indicate about Jewish attitudes toward life and death?

Family

CHAPTER SEVEN

"LIKE A PRISONER"

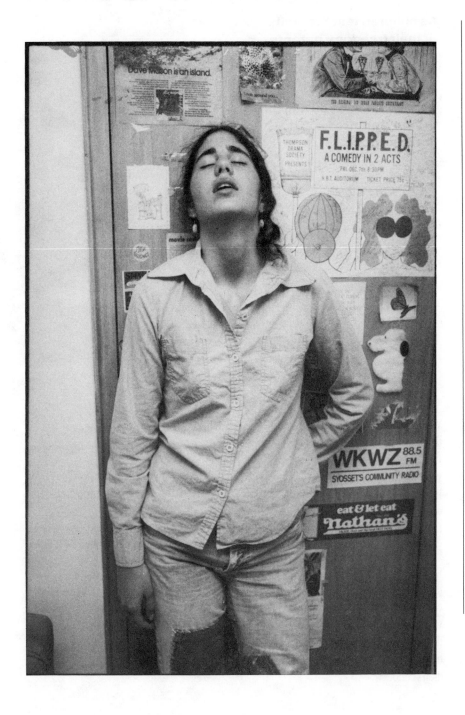

Family ties

Many families—perhaps even most—embody positive and wholesome relationships between parents and children and among brothers and sisters. Tensions and problems are handled smoothly, in an atmosphere of cooperation, respect, and love. If you are lucky enough to be part of such a family, reading about Sam may help you appreciate your good fortune.

Sam has so many complaints about his parents he scarcely knows where to begin or end. He has had six sessions with the psychologist to whom they sent him.

Again and again, with mounting anger, he says: "They make me feel like a prisoner. . . . I'm hemmed in on all sides, with no freedom. . . . I'm nearly eighteen years old, but they control me even more than they do my eleven-year-old sister. . . . Everything she does is cute, everything I do is wrong. . . . Sometimes I wish my parents were dead. Then I get to feel guilty about that, and I can't tell whether I'm angrier at them or myself."

Would you have more freedom or less if there were no rules governing your home life?

When pressed for specifics, Sam says he resents the fact that before he goes out on a date or even to spend a couple of hours with the guys in the evening, he has to tell his parents exactly where he's going and with whom. A couple of times his mother even phoned the home he said he'd be visiting to check up on him. If he isn't back from a date by midnight, he's grounded for a month.

Of course, Sam's parents see things quite differently. They say that Sam has been stubborn and willful since early childhood. They're afraid his friends may lead him into all kinds of bad habits, including the use of alcohol and drugs. "Sam has a lot of potential," they say, "but very little will power or sense of direction. He needs us to point the way."

Rules

What is your opinion of the rules and restrictions Sam's parents impose? Are they too lenient? Too strict? Reasonable and proper?

From time to time, all of us resent the fact that our freedom is curbed by rules. Yet what would life be like without rules? Suppose you could do anything you wanted while playing baseball: run the bases backward, get four strikes at bat, steal a base on a foul ball—ignore the rules whenever you felt like it. What would happen to the game? Suppose we could drive our cars on the right or the left side of the road, at any particular moment we saw fit and at whatever speed we wanted. Would we have more or less freedom under these conditions?

As children test the limits of their freedom, parents need to provide not only discipline but also comfort, reassurance, and love. To what extent do you still turn to your parents for emotional support?

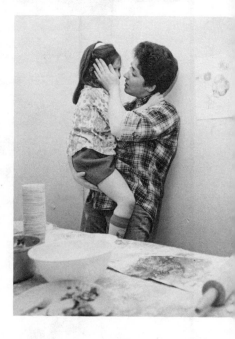

Would you have more freedom or less if there were no rules governing your family life? Which of your parents' rules do you think are necessary and fair? Which, if any, are neither? Why? Which rules would you like to suggest your parents follow? Have you ever discussed this with them?

Do you feel your parents were fair in disciplining you when you were a little child? Fair now? Too strict? Too lenient? When should parents stop disciplining their children? When should they stop trying to influence or direct their children's conduct?

Deadly discipline

A passage in the Torah has long posed a problem for Jewish commentators:

If a man has a disloyal and defiant son, who does not heed his father or mother and does not obey them even after they discipline him, his father and mother shall take hold of him and bring him out to the elders of his town at the public place of his community. . . . Thereupon the men of his town shall stone him to death.

Deuteronomy 21:18-21

Did this passage surprise and upset you? If so, you are not alone. This biblical commandment bothered our ancient rabbis, too. Yet what could they do about it? After all, they believed the Torah to be literally the word of God, and they could not abrogate or annul the word of God.

The rabbis handled this situation as they did so many others. They left the Torah law as it was—inviolate, unchanged—but surrounded it with so many conditions and restrictions that it was, for all practical purposes, inoperative.

Scripture speaks of a "stubborn and rebellious son." This refers to a son . . . but not a full-grown man. Yet a minor [under the age of thirteen] is exempt from the penalty, since he is not responsible for upholding the commandments. . . .

If the father [of one who is old enough to be responsible] wants him punished, but not his mother, or the reverse, he is not treated as a "stubborn and rebellious son."

Mishnah Sanhedrin 8:1-5

But [the stoning of a son] never happened and never will happen. Why then was this law written? That you may study it and receive reward.

Sanhedrin 71a

If a man beats his child, he is placed under a ban, because he may be causing his child to sin by rebelling against him.

Maimonides, Mishneh Torah, Kibud Av V'aim, *chap. 6*

Growing

Although they don't say so explicitly, the ancient teachers of Judaism seemed to recognize that each person grows through various stages of development and must be treated accordingly.

How much must parents or caretakers do for an infant? How much can the infant do for itself? Should parents allow the baby total freedom to crawl wherever it wants or put anything it wants in its mouth? On the other hand, should parents keep watch over the infant at all times and completely discourage the baby from experimenting and reaching for things?

Even at the earliest stages of growth, discipline— sometimes even punishment—is required, but it should be loving, gentle, and fair. Our ancient teachers understood this:

Abraham and Isaac: a nineteenth-century Italian engraving.

When God ordered Abraham to sacrifice Isaac (Genesis 22:1-19), was that a fair test of Abraham's faith? In what sense might some of today's parents be accused of "sacrificing" their children?

How much freedom should parents allow young children to experiment and explore?

At eighteen you will be old enough to vote, old enough to drive a car, old enough to serve in the military. In what ways might you still be dependent on your parents?

If you strike a child, strike him only with a shoelace.

Baba Batra 21a

Do you believe parents should ever use physical force in punishing a child? If so, what kinds of physical punishment are appropriate? What kinds are excessive? If you think physical punishment is never appropriate, what form of discipline would you recommend? Should the type of punishment vary with the age of the child and the nature of the wrongdoing? If so, how? How can we distinguish appropriate discipline from child abuse?

Tug of war

The relationship between parents and their growin children has been compared to a tug of war. Do you agree? At what period in a child's life do discipline and authority dominate? When does the pull of freedom become the more powerful force? Which Jewish ritual signifies the transition from childhood dependency to adult responsibility?

When you first entered adolescence, you were obviously less dependent on your parents than you were as an infant. You could feed yourself and in many ways protect yourself against danger without parental supervision. It would be foolish to pretend, however, that at age thirteen—or, for that matter, even today —all parental authority, discipline, and protection can be eliminated. In earlier times, a thirteen-year-old might already be contributing significantly to household income and might even be ready for be-

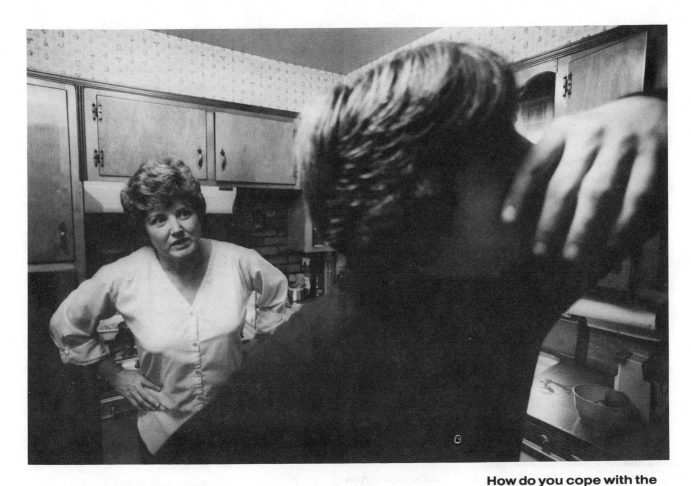

trothal. Today, because our society is more sophisticated technologically and requires so much more education, at age thirteen—or sixteen or eighteen—you are likely to be much more dependent on your elders than were your grandparents and great-grandparents at that age.

By age eighteen to twenty-one you will be almost fully adult—physically mature and ready to graduate from college, to vote, to serve in the military. Yet, especially if you decide to study for a profession, you will most probably still be in school and still at least partly dependent on your parents.

Honor and fear

How does Jewish tradition regard the obligations children owe their parents?

Our rabbis taught: What is fear? ("Every man his mother and his father shall you fear.") "Fear" means the son must neither stand in his father's regular place nor sit in his regular seat nor contradict his words, nor side with his father's opponent in dispute when his father is present. "Honor" means that he must provide him with food and drink, clothe and cover him, lead him in and out.

Kiddushin 29a

Do you agree that a child should never contradict a parent's words or take the opposing side in an argument when others are present? To what extent does the ancient rabbinic concept of the father's role in the household differ from the one that prevails today?

How do you cope with the tension and conflict that develop as relationships change?

67

It was asked of Rabbi Ulla, "How far must one go in giving honor to parents?" He replied: "Consider what a certain heathen named Dama son of Nathina did in Askelon. The sages once desired merchandise from him on which he would make a profit of 600,000 gold dinarim. But the key to the room in which the merchandise was kept was lying under his sleeping father, and he would not trouble him in order to complete the transaction."

Ibid

Which of the above restrictions on your behavior would you accept? Which would you reject? Why? Do you think the actions the rabbis described truly show honor to parents? Love? Respect?

Parents and God

There are three partners in the creation of [a person]: God and father and mother.

Kiddushin 30b

Great is the honor one owes one's parents—for God raises it even above the honor one owes Him.

In one place it says: "Honor your father and your mother (Exodus 20:12)." In another it says: "Honor the Lord with your substance . . . (Proverbs 3:9)."

How do you honor God? With the wealth in your possession. . . . If you do not have the means, you are not obliged.

But with "Honor your father and your mother" it is not so; whether you have the means or not, honor your father and your mother, even if you must become a beggar at the door.

Jerusalem Kiddushin 1:7

Do you agree that you owe even more homage and respect to your parents than to God? Would this be true of all parents? Of none? Why? How may love and respect for your parents lead to love and respect for God? How may love and respect for God lead to similar feelings toward your parents? Are you comfortable with prayers that refer to God as "Father"? Why or why not?

Are parents always right?

In a tradition as family oriented as Judaism, you might expect that people your age would be expected to do whatever their parents wanted. If so, you would be wrong.

Everything which your parent says to you, you are required to obey. But if your parent says to you, "Let us bow down to idols," you must not obey lest you become an apostate.

Yalkut Mishle 960

Question: Is a father permitted to prevent his son from migrating to the Land of Israel?

Answer: Because it is a mitzvah to go to the land of Israel . . . the son need not obey his father. The honor of the Lord ranks above all.

Rabbi Meir of Rothenberg

How can you reconcile the apparent contradiction between Rabbi Meir's response and the previous passage from the Jerusalem Talmud?

If one's father directed him to violate a commandment of the Torah . . . he need not listen.

Shulḥan Arukh, Yoreh De'ah 240:15

When a parent and child disagree, who decides whether a particular commandment of the Torah is or is not still bind-

Which Jewish ritual marks the transition from childhood dependency to adult responsibility? How much more independence do you have today than you had five years ago?

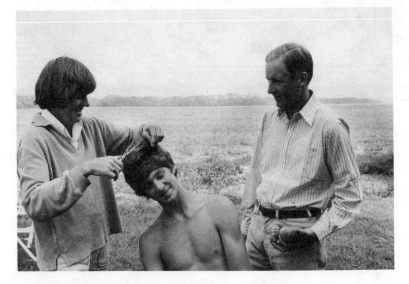

Parents and children need to take the time to learn from each other and share each other's company. What activities do you and your parents enjoy together?

ing? Can you think of a specific situation in which, according to the Torah, a child might be justified in refusing to obey a parent? A situation in which such disobedience would not be justified?

Suppose a man is on trial for cheating on his income tax return. He orders his daughter, who works for him, to testify falsely, in order to save him from a probable conviction and prison sentence. What should the daughter do? What is her obligation to her father? To the teachings of the Torah? To the government? To herself? Would the situation be any different if the daughter were under indictment and asked her father to testify falsely in order to protect her?

Eleventh Commandment

It has been suggested that the following might make a good Eleventh Commandment: "You shall honor your daughter and your son." Do you agree? Why or why not? If there were such a commandment, how would you rate your parents in observing it? Do you think you have done reasonably well in observing the Fifth Commandment: "Honor your father and your mother"? What effect, if any, might this proposed Eleventh Commandment have on observance of the fifth?

Was God's favoritism to Abel partly to blame for Cain's act of violence against him?

Sibling rivalry

Let's go back to Sam's complaint about his parents' favoritism toward his sister: "They control me even more than they do my eleven-year-old sister. . . . Everything she does is cute, everything I do is wrong."

A quick look at Jewish tradition will disclose how old the problem of sibling rivalry really is.

Now Israel loved Joseph best of all his sons, for he was the child of his old age; and he made him an ornamented tunic. And when his brothers saw that their father loved him more than any of his brothers, they hated him so that they could not speak a friendly word to him.

Genesis 37:3-4

A man should never single out one son among his others, for on account of [the ornamented tunic] that Jacob gave Joseph . . . , his brothers became jealous of him.

Shabbat 10b

What was Jacob's motivation in making an ornamented tunic for Joseph? Can parents always avoid favoritism in the treatment of their children? Are children always correct in suspecting favoritism on the part of their parents? Can you think of any other biblical stories portraying a parent's favoritism for one child over another?

In the course of time, Cain brought an offering to the Lord from the fruit of the soil; and Abel, for his part, brought the choicest of the firstlings of his flock.

The Lord paid heed to Abel and his offering, but to Cain and his offering he paid no heed. Cain was much distressed and his face fell. . . .

And when they were in the field, Cain set upon his brother Abel and killed him.

Genesis 4:3-5, 8

The selection from Genesis seems to blame God—doesn't it?—for Cain's sin in killing his brother: God's favoritism to Abel, like Jacob's favoritism to Joseph, caused the sibling rivalry that led to violence. How is such a charge possible, even by implication? Isn't God supposed to be perfect?

Brothers on a hill

Our tradition also contains examples of warm, loving relationships between siblings.

Legend has it that two brothers were farmers. One lived with his wife and children on one side of a hill, and the other, unmarried, lived in a small hut on the other side of the hill.

One year the brothers had an especially good harvest. The married brother looked over his fields and thought to himself: "God has been good to me. I have a wife and children and more crops than I need. I am so much better off than my brother, who lives all alone. Tonight, while my brother is asleep, I will carry some of my sheaves to his field. When he finds them tomorrow, he'll never suspect they came from me."

On the other side of the hill, the unmarried brother looked at his harvest and thought to himself: "God has been kind

to me. But I wish He had been as good to my brother. His needs are so much greater than mine. He must feed his wife and children, yet I have just as much food and grain as he has. Tonight, while my brother and his family are asleep, I will place some of my sheaves in his field. Tomorrow, when he finds them, he'll never know I placed them there."

So both brothers waited patiently until midnight. Then each loaded his grain on his shoulders and walked up the hill. Exactly at midnight they met each other at the summit. Realizing that each had thought only of helping the other, the two brothers embraced and cried with joy.

If you have any brothers and sisters, how would you rate your relationship? How has it changed over the years? Do you ever feel jealousy or anger toward each other? When do you most enjoy each other's company? Are you able to share confidences about matters you have trouble discussing with your parents?

Tension and change

As you grow—and your relationship to your family changes—a certain amount of tension is normal. Learning how to handle it is important preparation for living harmoniously with larger groups of people whose opinions and desires differ from your own. An important key to maturity is allowing relationships to develop slowly and regularly. Parents must be ready to yield—and children to

Can your family resolve disagreements in an atmosphere of respect, cooperation, and love?

accept— more responsibility and freedom year by year, even month by month. Parental control is much like a dam; unless there are sluices through which some water can flow at all times, pressure may build up to the point of destructive collapse.

Resolving the tension between generations would be difficult even in a stable environment. But ours is not a stable environment. We live at a time when values and behavior are changing rapidly. Thirty years ago it was highly unusual for a couple to live together before marriage; today it seems quite common. Thirty years ago homosexuality was mentioned, if at all, only behind closed doors; today it is discussed openly and freely.

How can parents and children resolve such generational differences? Not easily. A good way to start is for parents not to assume that the old way is right just because it's old, and for young people not to take it for granted that everything new

is correct just because it's new. Each must strive (easier said than done!) to see things through the eyes of the other. How would I feel about this if I were my mother . . . father . . . daughter . . . son? Suppose time proves me to be only partially right, or even largely wrong? How can we successfully live together, neither surrendering, neither dictating?

Your parents faced these kinds of problems long before you were born, in their relationship with your grandparents. Your children will confront similar problems as their relationship develops with you. There are no sure or easy answers. My profoundest hope is that the wisdom of our ancestors, combined with your most serious thought, will help you arrive at your own personal and creative solutions, which will then enrich the heritage of generations to come.

CHAPTER EIGHT

COUNTING OUR DAYS

Adjusting to change

The discussion of change that concludes Chapter Seven may be even more relevant to your relationships with your grandparents than with your parents. I can remember a time when there was no television or even radio, when calculators and computers and spaceships and nuclear missiles were science fiction rather than fact. To my grandchildren, all these are quite commonplace. Who knows what more drastic and dramatic changes lie just beyond the horizon?

Some elders can accept such radical novelty with relative ease; others find this kind of acceptance difficult, even impossible. Your vital first step in establishing good relationships with your grandparents is to appreciate the enormous, sometimes bewildering changes to which they have had to adjust.

How would you rate your relationships with your grandparents? Have they changed for better or worse in the past two or three years? Do any of your grandparents live with you? If so, what difference does that make in your relationship? Do you see enough of your grandparents? Too much? Not enough?

How would you compare your and your parents' relationships with your grandparents? Who seems to get along better?

People need to feel they control their own lives. What changes—physical, social, mental, emotional—can make elderly people feel vulnerable? What can we do to help them feel more secure?

Positive attitude

Once the emperor Hadrian was walking along the road near Tiberias in Galilee, and he saw an old man working the soil to plant some fig trees.

"If you had worked in your early years, old man," he said, "you would not have to work now so late in your life."

"I have worked both early and late," the man answered, "and what pleased the Lord He has done with me."

"How old are you?" asked Hadrian.

"A hundred years old," the man answered.

"A hundred years old, and you still stand there breaking up the soil to plant trees!" said Hadrian. "Do you expect to eat the fruit of those trees?"

"If I am worthy, I will eat," said the old man. "But if not, as my father worked for me, I work for my children."

Leviticus Rabbah 25:15

Rabbi Naḥman once asked Rabbi Isaac to bless him as they were saying goodbye. Rabbi Isaac replied:

"Let me give you a parable. A man traveled a long way in the desert. He felt hungry, weary, and thirsty, when suddenly he came upon a tree filled with sweet fruits, covered with branches that provided delightful shade, and watered by a brook that flowed nearby.

What leads these men to plant and build for a future they may never see?

"The man rested in the tree's shade, ate of its fruits, and drank its water. When he was about to leave, he turned to the tree and said:

"'O tree, beautiful tree, with what shall I bless you? Shall I wish that your shade be pleasant? It is already pleasant. Shall I say that your fruits should be sweet? They are sweet. Shall I ask that a brook flow by you? A brook does flow by you. Therefore I will bless you this way: May it be God's will that all the shoots taken from you be just like you.'

"So it is with you," Rabbi Isaac said to Rabbi Naḥman. "What can I wish you? Shall I wish you learning? You have learning. Wealth? You have wealth. Children? You have children.

"Therefore I say: May it be God's will that all your offspring be like you."

Ta'anit 5b-6a

What kinds of things can you learn from your grandparents? What kinds of things can your grandparents learn from you? Which of your grandparents' traits would you like to have? Which would you rather not have?

Proper respect

Elders sometimes feel rejected and scorned by the younger members of their families, treated disdainfully because they are no longer as energetic and active as they once were. Children, on the other hand, sometimes resent what they perceive to be the desire of their grandparents to control them, to dictate their behavior by standards that now seem old-fashioned.

Judaism has always expressed great respect for the elderly:

A man must not dishonor his father in his speech. How so? For example, if the father is old and wants to eat early in the morning, as old men do, and asks his son for food, and the son says, "The sun has not yet risen, and you're already up and want to eat!?"

Or when the father says, "My son, how much did you pay for this coat or for the food you brought me?" And the son answers, "I bought it and paid for it. It isn't your business to ask the price!"

Or when he thinks to himself, "When will this old man die, so I may be free of what he costs me?"

Israel ben Joseph Al-Nakawa, Menorat ha-Ma'or, *chap. 4, p. 16*

In what ways can we show proper respect to the elderly? Would a prosperous son who failed to provide his needy parent with food and clothing be showing proper respect? How about a well-to-do daughter who sent a generous check each month but had as little personal contact as possible with her elderly parent?

Do any of your grandparents live at home with you? If so, they are the exception: increasingly, the elderly—at least, those who can afford to—move to retirement communities in Florida, Arizona, and elsewhere. What problems and opportunities does this trend suggest?

Among the storks, the old birds stay in their nests when they can no longer fly, while the young ones fly over sea and land, gathering from everywhere provisions for the needs of their elders. . . .

With this example before them, may not human beings who take no thought for their parents deservedly hide their faces for shame?

Philo Judaeus, On the Decalogue, *secs. 115-118*

You shall rise before the aged and show deference to the old; you shall revere your God; I am the Lord.

Leviticus 19:32

The first words of the quotation from Leviticus are inscribed in each car of the mountain subway in Haifa. They are meant to encourage younger riders to offer their seats to older passengers. Our tradition recognizes, however, that such courtesies can be extended lovingly or in a manner that actually humiliates the recipient.

There was a man who used to feed his father fattened chickens. Once his father said to him, "My son, where did you get these chickens?" He answered, "Old man, shut up and eat, just as dogs shut up when they eat!" Such a man feeds his father on fattened chickens but inherits Gehenna [hell]. . . .

There was another man who worked in a mill. The king ordered that millers be brought to work for him. The man said to his father, "You stay here and work in the mill in my place. I will go to work for the king. For if any harm comes to the king's workers, I prefer that it fall on me, not on you. . . ."

Such a man puts his father to work treading a mill, yet inherits the Garden of Eden.

Jerusalem Kiddushin 1:7

What lesson can you draw from this selection concerning proper behavior toward grandparents? What advice can you offer grandparents concerning the respect they owe their grandchildren?

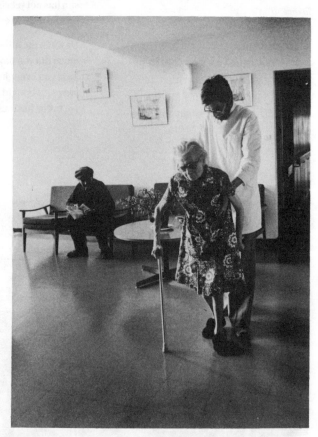

How well do your grandparents cope with their physical infirmities? What can you do to make their lives easier?

Infirmities of age

You have most probably noticed from your own grandparents or great-grandparents that as we grow older, we are likely to suffer certain physical impairments. We no longer move with the energy and agility we once had; it requires greater effort to accomplish less.

It is natural for old people to be despised by the general population when they can no longer function as they once did, but sit idle, and have no purpose. The commandment "Honor your father and your mother" was given specifically for this situation.

Gur Aryeh ha-Levi, Malekhet Mahshevet, *commentary on the Fifth Commandment*

Do you agree that the elderly are "despised by the general population"? Do you feel society in general treats old people fairly? Some people say our movies, music, literature, and advertising glorify the young. Do you agree? What effect might this have on the way old people are treated? On the image the elderly have of themselves?

Rabbi Yose ben Kisma said: Woe for the one thing that goes and does not return.

What is that?

One's youth.

Rabbi Dimi said: Youth is a crown of roses, old age a crown of heavy willow rods.

Shabbat 152a

Do you consider youth always to be a "crown of roses"? Ask your grandparents or others of comparable age whether they view their longevity as "a crown of heavy willow rods." If you could be any age right now, which would you choose? Why?

So appreciate your vigor in the days of your youth, before those days of sorrow come and those years arrive of which you will say, "I have no pleasure in them"; before sun and light and moon and stars grow dark, and the clouds come back after the rain:

When the guards of the house become shaky,

And the men of valor are bent,

And the maids that grind, grown few, are idle,

And the ladies that peer through the windows grow dim,

And the doors to the street are shut—

With the noise of the hand mill growing fainter,

And the song of the bird growing feebler,

And all the strains of music dying down;

When one is afraid of heights

And there is terror on the road. . . .

Before the silver cord snaps

And the golden bowl crashes,

The jar is shattered at the spring,

And the jug is smashed at the cistern.

And the dust returns to the ground

As it was,

And the lifebreath returns to God

Who bestowed it.

Ecclesiastes 12:1-7

In the selection from Ecclesiastes, what, specifically, do the following phrases mean?

■ "When the guards of the house become shaky"

■ "The maids that grind, grown few, are idle"

■ "The ladies that peer through the windows grow dim"

■ "The song of the bird growing feebler"

■ "The golden bowl crashes"

Do these metaphors fit your grandparents? If so, how do they cope? If not, how can you explain the discrepancies?

Coping

**The span of our life is seventy years,
or, given the strength, eighty years;
but the best of them are trouble and
sorrow.
They pass by speedily, and we are in
darkness. . . .
Teach us to count our days rightly,
that we may obtain a wise heart.**

Psalms 90:10-12

Is there anything in these words that
might be changed if they were being
written today? At your age, how can you
"count [your] days rightly"? Your grandparents at their age?

Sometimes we can understand what appears to be strange behavior in older
people by realizing that they may be trying
to compensate for feelings of inadequacy.
A Jewish anthropologist, writing about
senior citizens in a center near Los Angeles, put it this way:

Among people so helpless, so vulnerable, so needy, the loss of control was
extraordinarily threatening. Their efforts were directed at convincing others, and then themselves, that they were
in charge of their life. . . . Underlying
this was the unspoken, enormous fear
of senility. . . . A forgotten word, an outburst of temper, a non sequitur, a mis-
placed object, a lapse of judgment or
reasoning were all scrutinized as omi-
nous portents that the process of decay
was beginning. At odds with this desire
for self-control was their attraction to
intensity, interpreted by them as an in-
dication that one was still fully alive.
. . . Passion was a sign of continuing
strength and involvement. Fierce activity and feelings proved that their pow-
ers were intact. They were read as evidence of vitality and used to counter
the dimming of physical sensation that
everyone experienced to some degree.
. . . Thus, old people were in a double
bind for which there was no solution—
pulled toward poise and dignity by one
need, and pulled toward outburst and
passion by the other.

Barbara Myerhoff, Number Our Days *(Dutton,
1978), p. 181*

Have you ever observed in the elderly the
kind of conduct described here? How do
people your own age sometimes behave
in order to mask their feelings of inadequacy? Why do people sometimes display more hostility toward their closest
relatives—sons, daughters, siblings, parents, mates—than toward strangers?

**According to Genesis,
Methusaleh lived 969
years—a tradition in keeping with the ancient belief
that great people lived to a
great age. How does this
attitude toward old age differ from the one that prevails in our society?**

Advantages of age

In describing the infirmities often endured
by older people, we have considered only
half the truth. Men and women your
grandparents' age also enjoy certain advantages. They have lived long enough to
correct some of their earlier mistakes, to
realize that perhaps the goals they pursued so assiduously in their youth were
not the most important ones after all.
They may also have developed more acceptance of and patience with lifestyles
and opinions different from their own.
Moreover, they may be less preoccupied
than your parents with the tensions of
running a business or competing for social standing.

Perhaps this is why some young people
develop a deep appreciation of the needs
and feelings of the elderly. Here is a folk
tale Barbara Myerhoff heard from one of
the older women at the Los Angeles center:

**Once there was a rich man who decided
he would give all his money to his son
as soon as the boy was grown instead of
following the custom of making the boy
wait till the father's death to inherit. He
did this, but soon the son began to ne-
glect his elderly father, and one day the
son put him out of the house. The old
man left and came back many years later.
He saw his little grandson playing outside the house and told the child who
he was. "Fetch me a cloak, child," he
said, "because I am cold and poor." The
little boy rummaged in the attic for an
old cloak and was cutting it in half when
his father came in. "What are you doing,
child?" he asked. "Father, I am going to
give half of the cloak to my grandfather
and keep the other half for you, for the
time when I am grown up and you have
grown old."**

Ibid., p. 20

To whom do you feel closer, your parents
or your grandparents? Who do you think
understands you better? With whom do
you feel freer to talk about your feelings,
hopes, and fears?

Young and old people often feel a special bond. What do you and your grandparents most enjoy doing together?

Balancing

A great twentieth-century Jewish thinker has summarized impressively both the advantages and disadvantages of growing older:

According to all the standards we employ . . . the aged person is condemned as inferior. . . . Conditioned to operating as a machine for making and spending money, with all other relationships dependent upon its efficiency, the moment the machine is out of order and beyond repair, one begins to feel like a ghost without a sense of reality. . . . Regarding himself as a person who has outlived his usefulness, he feels as if he has to apologize for being alive.

May I suggest that man's potential for change and growth is much greater than we are willing to admit, and that old age be regarded not as the age of stagnation but *as the age of opportunities for inner growth*.

The years of old age . . . are indeed formative years, rich in possibilities to unlearn the follies of a lifetime, to see through inbred self-deceptions, to deepen understanding and compassion, to widen the horizons of honesty, to refine the sense of fairness.

Abraham Joshua Heschel, "To Grow in Wisdom," Judaism *(Spring 1977)*

To what extent do your grandparents display the advantages of age? The disadvantages? Can you think of ways you can plan now to make your later years happier and more fulfilling? Heschel implies that the early and middle years of a person's life should be devoted to acquisition and accomplishment, the later years to inner growth. Do you agree? Why or why not?

A continuing role

You probably knew even before reading this chapter that as men and women grow older, and retire from their vocations or professions, they risk losing the self-respect that comes with fulfilling definite functions in their families and society. It is important, therefore, that as people grow older, they take on significant new roles, so they continue to feel needed. Depending on the health, interests, and abilities of the people involved, such new roles might include tending a family garden, planning shopping lists and menus, handling the family budget, aiding in the preparation of tax returns,

directing a family or community reading program and discussion group, and writing a family or community history or journal. What suggestions can you add to those listed here?

Respecting your grandparents and trying to help them doesn't mean that you must do things exactly as they do. This, too, was known to our ancestors:

After Rabbi Noah's succession as Rabbi at Lekhivitz, some Chasidim inquired of him: "Why do you not conduct yourself like your father, the late Rabbi?" "I do conduct myself like him," retorted Rabbi Noah. "He did not imitate anybody, and I likewise do not imitate anybody."

L. Newman and S. Spitz (eds.), The Hasidic Anthology *(Scribner's, 1935), p. 118*

Does nature put any age limit on love?

Promises

How can we understand or justify the conduct of the birds in the allegory that follows? Why was the answer of the third fledgling more acceptable than that of the first two? What light does this story shed on the obligations we owe our grandparents, our parents, and our children?

A bird once set out to cross a windy sea with his three fledglings. The sea was so wide and the wind so strong that the father bird was forced to carry his young, one by one, in his claws. When he was halfway across with his first fledgling, the wind turned to a gale, and he said, "My child, look how I am struggling and risking my life in your behalf. When you are grown up, will you do as much for me and provide for my old age?"

The fledgling replied, "Only bring me to safety, and when you are old I shall do everything you ask of me."

Whereat the father dropped his child into the sea, and it drowned, and he said, "So shall it be for such a liar as you."

Then the father bird returned to the shore, set forth with the second fledgling, asked the same question, and receiving the same answer, drowned the second child with the cry, "You, too, are a liar!"

Finally, he set out with the third fledgling, and when he asked the same question, the third and last fledgling replied:

"My dear father, it is true you are struggling mightily and risking your life in my behalf, and I shall be wrong not to repay you when you are old, but I cannot bind myself. This, though, I can promise: when I am grown up and have children of my own, I shall do as much for them as you have done for me."

Whereupon the father bird said, "Well spoken, my child, and wisely; your life I will spare and I will carry you to safety."

Glueckel of Hameln, Memoirs

A father's love is for his children; the children's love is for their own children.

Sotah 49a

Is this statement from the Talmud true? What effect, if any, does substituting the word ''mother'' or ''parent'' for ''father'' have on its validity? Does the statement declare (a) what is, (b) what ought to be, or (c) what should be rejected?

CHAPTER NINE

IN THE SHADOW OF A CLOUD

Tensions

Joan can't remember a time when her home was really peaceful. Her earliest memories are of her parents' bickering and shouting. She remembers locking herself in her room and burying her head in a pillow to shut out the noise of their frequent arguments. When they weren't screaming at each other, they weren't communicating at all. Sometimes for several days their only verbal contact was in the form of notes they would leave for each other on a table or dresser.

The constant tension has so scarred Joan that she has vowed never to marry. "Not for a million dollars," she says, "would I ever inflict anything like this on any child of mine! I feel as if I'm living in the shadow of a cloud which no wind can blow away."

Do you know a married couple that resembles Joan's parents? Can you think of anything Joan might do to help them? Do you think Joan is right in rejecting the idea of marriage?

How would you rate your parents' marriage? Excellent? Good? Pretty good? Poor? Are they divorced? So far as you

To what extent do the families you know resemble this "typical" American family of the 1950s? Were American families ever really like this?

know, have they ever considered divorce? When and if you marry, in what ways would you like your marriage to be like that of your parents? In what ways would you like it to be different?

Divorce

It shouldn't surprise you to learn that Joan's parents were finally divorced. The court fight was bitter and nasty. Not least among the issues the couple fought over was custody of Joan and her brother. The judge's decision: the children were to live with their mother during the week, with their father over the weekends and for a month each summer. Mother is a strict disciplinarian. Father lets Joan do just about anything she wants. Each parent, moreover, is always asking her for information about the other, as if they expected her to spy for them. Joan feels like the rope in an emotional tug-of-war between her parents.

When a man acts at the bidding of his mother in the performance of a task which is displeasing to his father, he should not reveal to him that it was his mother who requested this act.

Sefer Ḥasidim 336

Is this sound advice? Doesn't it encourage Joan to lie to her parents? How can Joan avoid becoming a pawn in her parents' continuing conflict? How can Joan avoid the temptation to manipulate the conflict to her own advantage? Suppose that Joan's father has begun seeing another woman but doesn't want Joan's mother to know. How far should

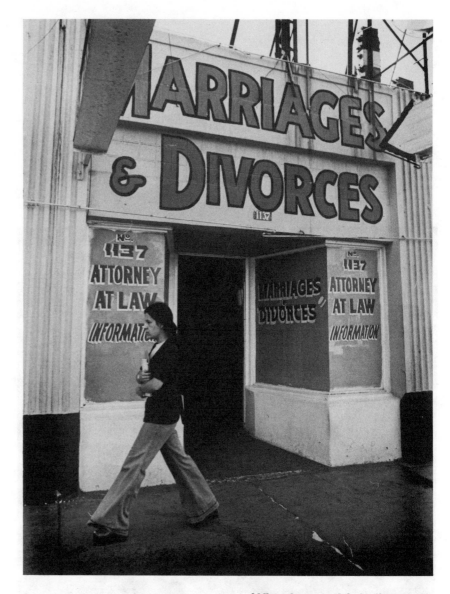

Joan be willing to stretch or suppress the truth in conversations with her mother in order to obey her father's wishes?

If you have experienced divorce in your immediate family, in your extended family, or in the families of your friends, how do your observations compare with Joan's case? How would you assess the direct impact of the divorce on the married couple? On their children? What about the long-term effect?

Why do you think divorce has become so widespread in American society? How have attitudes toward marriage and divorce changed since the time your grandparents got married?

Traditional Jewish attitudes

A bad wife is like leprosy to her husband. What is the remedy? Let him divorce her and be cured of his leprosy.

Yevamot 63b

A man takes a wife and possesses her. She fails to please him because he finds something obnoxious about her, and he writes her a bill of divorcement, hands it to her, and sends her away from his house.

Deuteronomy 24:1

According to this passage from Deuteronomy, who held the dominant role in marriage, the man or the woman? Did the fact that divorce was easier in Bible times work to the man's or the woman's advantage? Why?

Did you feel that either quotation was fair to wives? If you didn't, you are in good company. Many of our teachers sought to correct the apparent prejudice against women.

Rabbi Zusya's wife was unhappy in their marriage and persistently asked for a divorce. One night the rabbi called to her, "Hendel, look here." He showed her that his pillow was wet.

"The Talmud tells us that if a man divorces his first wife, the altar itself sheds tears. . . . My pillow is wet with those tears. Now do you still insist that we divorce?"

From then on, Rabbi Zusya's wife became happy and contented.

F. Klagsbrun, Voices of Wisdom *(Pantheon, 1980), p. 152*

How does the relationship between Zusya and his wife differ from the kind of marriage described in the two previous passages? Who originally asked for the divorce? How did Zusya persuade his wife that the marriage should remain intact? What was he really saying when he told her his pillow was wet with tears? What can we learn from the way Zusya and his wife resolved their differences?

The court may bring strong pressure upon the husband until he says, "I am willing to divorce my wife."

Arakhin 5:6

If a woman says, "My husband is distasteful to me, I cannot live with him," the court compels the husband to divorce her, because a wife is not a captive.

Maimonides, Yad Ishut, *14:8*

In each of these two passages, who has requested the divorce? Whose rights is the court protecting?

After reviewing what our authorities have said about divorce, several conclusions become apparent:

1. Biblical and talmudic law on divorce clearly favors husbands over wives.

2. Some authorities were so uncomfortable with this that they sought to protect the rights of wives.

3. A strict interpretation of rabbinic law still puts women at a decided disadvantage in most divorce cases.

4. This disadvantage is increased by the fact that, as I write this, all rabbinic courts involving more than Reform and Reconstructionist rabbis have consisted entirely of men.

Parents and children

[T]he traditional law makes a distinction between custody of a boy child and custody of a girl child. The distinction is based upon the fact that according to the old traditional law, the duty of studying the Torah was incumbent upon a boy and not upon a girl and that, furthermore, the obligation to teach the Torah (or to provide for the instruction) is an obligation incumbent upon the father and not upon the mother.

Because of these two facts, the traditional law of custody works out as follows: Infant children are in the custody of their mother. A girl child is permanently in the custody of the mother. A boy child can be claimed by the father after he reaches the age of six because at that age he must begin the study of the Torah.

S. B. Freehof, Current Reform Responsa *(Hebrew Union College Press, 1969), pp. 193f*

Was this a reasonable solution when it was originally proposed? Is it reasonable now? Why?

Even under the best of circumstances, a child of divorced parents is in a difficult situation. The greater the animosity and acrimony between the parents, the more painful will be the child's dilemma. In answer to the question "How do I deal with my parents' divorce?" I offered the following personal reflections:

I have two grandchildren whose parents are divorced. The disruption of my daughter's first marriage was very traumatic to her sons. Of one thing, however, they, she and I are firmly convinced: the crisis they had to confront was less damaging by far than the continuation

Raphael's *Judgment of Solomon.*

Caught in a tug-of-war between their parents, children in divorce proceedings may feel like the baby brought before Solomon in the Bible's most famous custody case. How do you think the courts should decide which parent gets custody of the children? To what extent should the children's own views be a deciding factor?

of a marriage which had already become quite meaningless. The healing which ensued would have been impossible without the surgery of divorce. I think I reflect accurately the following convictions of my grandsons in their relationship to their divorced parents:

1 My parents conceived me in love because they wanted me.

2 Both of my parents still love me, despite the fact that they have long ceased loving each other.

3 I still love both of my parents.

4 I will not criticize either of them in conversation with the other, nor will I allow either of them to express such criticism in my presence.

5 I am not responsible for the failure of their marriage.

Keeping Posted 30:6

Some parents who have fallen out of love agree to stay together "for the sake of the children." From your experience, which would you say does the children more harm: the dissolution or the continuation of a loveless marriage? Why?

Single-parent homes

If your parents are divorced or one of them has died, this section may address itself to some of your most urgent feelings. If you are among the fortunate majority of young people your age who live with both parents in happy homes, what follows may help you understand the problems faced by some of your friends.

Perhaps the first helpful thing for children of single-parent homes to realize is how much company they have. Between 1915 and 1985, the annual divorce rate in the United States increased by about 500 percent. Today, millions of Americans between the ages of ten and eighteen live with only one parent. Nearly half the babies now being born in the United States will probably live at least some part of their lives in a single-parent household.

Young people who have been separated from a parent by divorce tend to feel abandoned and fearful. If you ever endure (or have endured) such a separa-

tion, your feelings probably will (or did) resemble the responses to death we examined in Chapter Six. Any or all of these reactions are perfectly normal.

1. *Denial:* You refuse to accept the fact that the divorce has really occurred. You continue to express the hope that the marriage will somehow be repaired.

2. *Guilt:* Unrealistically and unfairly, you blame yourself for the breakup of your parents' marriage.

3. *Betrayal:* You feel deserted by those you love and depend on most for emotional security.

4. *Anger:* You blame your parents for getting the divorce.

5. *Fear:* You become anxious that one or both parents may abandon you or that financial woes may deprive you of things you want or need.

Because the single-parent home is a relatively new phenomenon, we find very little on the topic in traditional Jewish literature. Divorce was far less common in ancient and medieval times than it is now, and remarriage was encouraged after the death of a spouse. According to rabbinic law, a widower was permitted to remarry after the passage of only three festivals, which meant less than a year following the death of his wife. If, however, he had young children in need of maternal care, he could marry again after only thirty days. Even where such remarriage did not occur so soon, households were larger, so that there were others under the same roof to help care for the child.

What special burdens does the single-parent family place on both parent and child? What new difficulties arise when one or both of the divorced parents remarry?

Choosing a marriage partner

Our principal reason for examining in such detail the causes and consequences of divorce is to help you recognize the importance of choosing the right marriage partner. In fact, the choice of a marriage partner may well be the most important decision you will ever make.

You may make haste to buy property but you must pause and consider before taking a wife.

Yevamot 63a

A man should build himself a home, plant himself a vineyard and then bring into the home a bride.

Zohar Ḥadash 1:4b

Anxious moments at divorce court.

How would you assess the emotional and economic impact of divorce on the married couple? On their children? What about the long-term effects?

Can family therapy help to avert a marital breakup? What attitudes do both husband and wife need to bring to each session if therapy is to be effective?

To whom are these two statements addressed? How could they be rewritten to apply equally to both sexes? Why did our ancient teachers urge that a man should "build himself a home" before getting married? Were they thinking mainly in terms of money or personal comfort? If not, what did the metaphors of home and vineyard signify to them?

When do you expect to get married? In your teens? Your twenties? Your thirties? Researchers estimate that the divorce rate may be as much as six times higher in marriages where both husband and wife are under twenty-one than in marriages where both are over thirty-one. Why do you think this might be the case? What special problems and pressures are teenage married couples likely to face? Do people who marry as teenagers have any advantages over those who wait until their twenties or thirties?

Love, infatuation, romance

What does the word "love" mean to you? People can be said to love hot fudge sundaes, to love their parents, to love their husbands and wives, to love God. What, if anything, do these kinds of love have in common? In what ways do they differ?

How does love differ from romance? How does love differ from infatuation? How important a role should romance and sexual attraction play in courtship and marriage? What is likely to happen to a marriage that is based *solely* on romance and infatuation? What is likely to happen to a marriage in which the roles of romance and sexual attraction rapidly diminish?

What are the advantages of "going steady" with someone while you are still in your early or mid-teens? What are the disadvantages? How do you think you will best be able to distinguish between love, romance, and infatuation: by settling on one boyfriend or girlfriend at an early age, or by having a wide circle of friends and dating partners?

Knowing the difference

When you feel strongly attracted to someone in a romantic or sexual way, how can you tell whether you are experiencing love or merely infatuation? Asking yourself a few key questions may help you decide.

1. Is this the kind of person I would welcome as a friend? Would I want to spend a lot of time with this person even if there were no sexual attraction between us?

2. Does this person try to control and dominate me? Or does he or she encourage me to nurture and express my own capacities and views? Does this person try to satisfy my needs or mainly his or her own?

If your wife is short, bend down and whisper to her.

Baba Metzia 59a

Strive to fulfill your wife's wishes for that is equivalent to doing God's will.

A. B. Shoulson (ed.), Marriage and Family Life (Twayne, 1959), p. 62

And Abraham said to the senior servant of his household . . . , "Go to the land of my birth and get a wife for my son Isaac." . . . So the servant swore to him as bidden.

Then the servant . . . made his way to the city of Nahor. . . . And he said, "O Lord, God of my master Abraham. . . . As I stand here by the spring and the daugh-

What qualities will you look for in choosing a dating partner? Are they the same qualities you want in a husband or wife?

ters of the townspeople come out to draw water, let the maiden to whom I say, 'Please, lower your jar that I may drink,' and who replies, 'Drink, and I will also water your camels'—let her be the one whom You have decreed for Your servant Isaac."

Genesis 24:2-14

What mission did Abraham assign his senior servant? What criteria did the servant establish for choosing Isaac's wife? Do you think these criteria were appropriate? How might the young woman's behavior toward the servant and his camels indicate the kind of wife she would make for Isaac?

What criteria would you establish in choosing a wife or husband for yourself? For your best friend? How important are such criteria as looks, wealth, and popularity? What about kindness, generosity, intelligence, and religious commitment?

3. Is this person interested in the larger needs of humanity? Or is this person interested mainly in his or her immediate circle of family and friends?

There once lived a pious man who was childless. He prayed for a son, vowing to invite to his wedding feast every poor person in the city. A son was eventually born to him. . . . The boy grew up and his wedding day approached. The father invited all the students of the Torah and all the poor, who together filled six rooms.

God wished to test the bridegroom, and He sent the Angel of Death, in the guise of a man attired in soiled clothes, to beg for a place at the wedding. The bridegroom refused on the plea that all who could be accommodated had been invited. Moreover, the man's garments were objectionable.

In the night the Angel of Death revealed himself, declaring that he was about to take away the bridegroom's soul, since

he had failed the test. The bride gave voice to this prayer: "O Lord of the universe, You have said in Your Torah that, when a man takes to himself a wife, he shall bring her cheer for a full year and not leave her. May it be Your will that my husband live, and I shall teach him to practice lovingkindness to everyone without discrimination."

Her prayer was heard on high, and the Angel of Death was commanded to leave.

Midrash Aseret Hadibrot

Do you think it was fair for God to test the bridegroom, who had already paid to feed six rooms full of Torah students and poor people, by sending yet another beggar to the wedding? What did the test show about the limits of the man's generosity? Was he really interested in helping the poor, or only in fulfilling his earlier promise? Why might willingness to help the poor be a good indicator of suitability for marriage? What relationship, if any, does it bear to a willingness to nurture your interests and satisfy your needs? Is it possible for someone to be too interested in helping others and not attentive enough to his or her own needs?

4. How well matched are we intellectually? Are we similar in intelligence? Interested in the same kinds of cultural activities, such as reading, theater, and music?

A man ought always to strive to win in marriage the daughter of a Torah scholar and to give his daughter in marriage to a Torah scholar. If he cannot find the daughter of a Torah scholar, let him seek to marry the daughter of renowned communal leaders; if he cannot find one of these, let his choice be the daughter of a congregational leader; if not one of these, then the trustee of a charitable fund; if not one of these, let him select the daughter of an elementary Hebrew teacher, but let him not marry off his daughter to an ignorant man.

S. Kaplan and H. Ribalow, The Great Jewish Books (Horizon, 1952), p. 229

What does this paragraph show about the author's scale of values? About the values of the society for which he was writing? Who exercised the dominant role in seeking a marriage partner or choosing one for the child—men or women? Is this still true today? How might you rewrite the paragraph to make it more relevant to today's values and relationships?

In general, how important do you think it is for partners to be equally matched in intelligence? In educational attainment? All other things being equal, do you think you would be happier with a marriage partner whose taste in music and movies were similar to or different from yours?

5. How close in age are we?

If he was young and she old, or vice versa, they would say to him, "What sense is there in your marrying one much younger than yourself?" or, "What sense is there in your marrying one much older than yourself? Go, marry one who is about your own age and do not introduce strife into your house."

Yevamot 101b

How large does an age difference have to be before it jeopardizes a marriage? How important would a fifteen-year difference be when the persons involved are, respectively, twenty-five and ten years old? Fifty and thirty-five? Seventy-five and sixty?

What do you think are the most important attributes of a good marriage? Physical attraction? Religious commitment? Positive attitudes toward family life? What else do you think you'll need?

6. How similar are we in religious commitment? This question refers not only to formal religious affiliation (we'll talk more about that in the next chapter) but also to how important religious faith and practice are to each of us. A study published in the *Journal of Jewish Communal Service* (Winter 1984) reveals that couples who regularly take part in religious rituals together are six times less likely to be divorced than those who seldom share such rituals. Similarly, those who worship in synagogue at least once a week are four times more likely to remain married than those who do not.

Our ancient rabbis used an interesting play on words to emphasize the importance of religion in marriage. The Hebrew word for man is *ish*; for woman, *ishah*. The first word contains the letter *yod*, which is missing from the second; the second contains the letter *hay*, which does not appear in the first. These two letters together spell out a Hebrew abbreviation for God. If the *yod* and the *hay* are removed from *ish* and *ishah*, what remains in each case is the word *aysh*, meaning fire. From this, our ancient rabbis taught that when God is removed from the relationship between man and woman, nothing but consuming fire remains.

Why do you believe that couples who worship together are more likely to stay married than those who do not? Does their religious affiliation make them more fearful of how other people, their rabbi, or God will judge them? Are religious people more likely than other couples to equate divorce with failure? Or does their participation in religious rituals make them happier and reinforce the sense of sharing that keeps love alive?

Compatibility

The six questions we have just discussed all come under the heading of what is commonly called compatibility. The more compatible you and a prospective date are, the more fun you are likely to have together. And when the time for marriage approaches, the more compatible you and your prospective partner are, the greater is your chance for a happy and successful life together.

When should you start to pay attention to questions of compatibility? Before your first date with someone? After your first or second date? Not until you are seriously considering marriage? How much credence should you give to the old adage that "opposites attract"?

CHAPTER TEN

MIXED AND UNMATCHED

Barry's dates

Barry's parents have forbidden him to go out with girls who aren't Jewish. Because there have been mixed marriages in both their families, they seem determined to avoid that situation with their son.

''Take it easy!'' Barry has urged his parents during one of their arguments. ''You talk as if I'm getting married tomorrow. I'm sixteen years old and probably won't be ready to get married for ten years or more. I'm not that serious about any of the girls I've been dating. I just feel more comfortable with Gentile girls than with the Jewish girls I know. Don't make such a big deal over my high school dates!''

Barry complains that he is the only one in his crowd who isn't allowed to date Gentile girls. On several occasions he has done so despite his parents' prohibition, each time pledging his friends to secrecy. After such dates he has felt a strange combination of guilt and exhilaration at thwarting his parents' taboo.

It's easy for people to get married in Las Vegas. But how can they be sure they're making the right choice?

Couples come in all colors and religious affiliations. What effect do racial and religious differences have on the likely success of a marriage?

If you were Barry's parents, would you insist that he date only Jewish girls? If you were Barry, would you obey? Do you think Barry's parents are correct in their fear that dating Gentile girls will lead to a more serious involvement?

How large a part does religion play in your choice of friends? How significant a role do you think religion will have in your choice of dating partners? Do you think it's all right to go out on casual dates with non-Jewish partners? To ''go steady'' with a Gentile? To marry a non-Jew? Are there times when you feel more comfortable with your Gentile friends than with your Jewish friends? If yes, why do you think this is so?

Abraham amd Moses

Abraham was now old, advanced in years, and the Lord had blessed Abraham in all things. And Abraham said to the senior servant of his household, who had charge of all he owned, . . . "I will make you swear by the Lord, the God of heaven and the God of the earth, that you will not take a wife for my son from the daughters of the Canaanites among whom I dwell, but will go to the land of my birth and get a wife for my son Isaac."

Genesis 24:1-4

What reasons might Abraham have had for insisting that Isaac not marry a Canaanite woman? You may recall that before Isaac was born, Abraham took Sarah's Egyptian maidservant Hagar as

Ruth and Naomi.

Samson and Delilah.

If some of our greatest ancestors participated in mixed marriages, why do so many Jewish authorities condemn the practice?

Moses among the Midianites.

his concubine, and they had a son, Ishmael. Was Abraham being hypocritical in preventing Isaac from doing something Abraham himself had done? What event that happened between the birth of Ishmael and the birth of Isaac might have changed Abraham's outlook? What relation, if any, do you see between Abraham's insistence that Isaac not marry a Canaanite and his forcing Hagar and Ishmael out of his household? Would marrying among the Canaanites have made Isaac more or less likely to maintain Abraham's covenant with God?

The Bible explicitly tells us that Moses married more than one Gentile woman:

Now the priest of Midian had seven daughters. They came to draw water, and filled the troughs to water their father's flock; but shepherds came and drove them off. Moses rose to their defense, and he watered their flock. When they returned to their father, Reuel, he said, "How is it that you have come back so soon today?" They answered, "An Egyptian rescued us from the shepherds; what is more, he drew water for us and watered the flock." He said to his daughters, "Where is he then? Why did you leave the man? Ask him to break bread." Moses consented to stay with the man, and he gave Moses his daughter Zipporah as wife.

Exodus 2:16-21

When they were in Hazeroth, Miriam and Aaron spoke against Moses because of the Cushite [black] woman he had married. . . .

The Lord came down in a pillar of cloud, stopped at the entrance of the tent, and called out "Aaron and Miriam!" The two of them came forward; and He said, ". . . My servant Moses . . . is trusted throughout My household. With him I speak mouth to mouth, plainly and not in riddles, and he beholds the likeness of the Lord. How then did you not shrink from speaking against my servant Moses!" Still incensed with them, the Lord departed.

As the cloud withdrew from the Tent, there was Miriam stricken with snow-white scales!

Numbers 12:1-10

In Deuteronomy, however, when Moses addresses the Israelites, he cautions against intermarriage:

When the Lord your God brings you to the land that you are about to invade and occupy. . . [y]ou shall not intermarry with them: do not give your daughters to their sons or take their daughters for your sons; for they will turn your children away from me to worship other gods.

Deuteronomy 7:1, 3-4

Was Moses being hypocritical in urging his people not to marry non-Jews, even though he himself had done so? What important historical event made the Israelites' situation at the time of Deuteronomy very different from when Moses married Zipporah? Do you see any similarity between Abraham's instructions to his senior servant and Moses' instructions to the Israelites? What specific reason does Moses give for cautioning against intermarriage? Can you think of any episode in the Bible that shows us why Moses might have feared that his people's faith in God was not as strong as his had been? In what sense is Moses' warning still true today?

Examples and prohibitions

Once Samson went down to Timnah; and while in Timnah, he noticed a girl among the Philistine women. On his return, he told his father and mother, "I noticed one of the Philistine women in Timnah; please get her for me as a wife." His father and mother said to him, "Is there no one among the daughters of your kinsmen and among all our people, that you must go and take a wife from the uncircumcised Philistines?" But Samson answered his father, "Get me that one, for she is the one that pleases me."

Judges 14:1-3

What does Samson's final demand show about his character? How would you describe his relationship with his parents? What implication should we draw from the famous biblical account of Samson's relationship with another non-Jewish woman, Delilah?

Consider the following passages from the books of Ezra and Ruth:

When all this was over, the officers approached me, saying, "The people of Israel . . . have not separated themselves from the peoples of the land whose abhorrent practices are like those of the Canaanites. . . . They have taken their daughters as wives for themselves and for their sons. . . ."

Now then, do not give your daughters in marriage to their sons or let their daughters marry your sons. . . . [L]et us make a covenant with our God to expel all these women, and those who have been born to them, in accordance with the bidding of the Lord. . . .

Ezra 9:1-2, 12; 10:3-4

Elimelech, Naomi's husband, died; and she was left with her two sons. They married Moabite women, one named Orpah and the other Ruth. . . . Then [her sons] also died. . . .

Accompanied by her two daughters-in-law, [Naomi] left the place where she had been living; and they set out on the road back to the land of Judah.

But Naomi said to her two daughters-in-law, "Turn back, each of you to your mother's house. . . . May the Lord grant that each of you find security in the house of a husband!" . . .

Orpah kissed her mother-in-law farewell. But Ruth clung to her. So she said, "See, your sister-in-law has returned to her people and her gods. Go follow your sister-in-law." But Ruth replied, "Do not urge me to leave you, to turn back and not follow you. For wherever you go, I will go; wherever you lodge, I will lodge; your people shall be my people, and your God my God. Where you die, I will die, and there I will be buried."

Ruth 1:3-17

You probably recognized the end of Ruth's response to Naomi. One of the most poetic of all biblical passages, it is read in the synagogue on Shavuot and is included to this day in the conversion ceremony whenever a Gentile woman chooses to become Jewish. How can you reconcile the story of Ruth with Moses' and Ezra's proclamations concerning intermarriage? How do the passages from Deuteronomy and Ruth differ in their assessment of

what happens when a Jew marries a non-Jew? Which outcome is more likely today? In view of the story of Ruth, do you think Ezra was too harsh in demanding the expulsion of all the women who had intermarried, along with their children? What historic circumstances led Ezra to demand such a drastic measure?

Jewish survival

Three major reasons explain why virtually all Jewish authorities and many Jewish parents oppose intermarriage.

The first is their fear for Jewish survival. Statistics indicate that the issue of Jewish survival is no less critical today than it was during the eras of Abraham, Moses,

and Ezra. During the Holocaust, six million Jews—more than one-third of the world's Jewish population—were murdered. Although the total population of the world more than doubled between 1939 and 1989, there were about as many Jews in 1989 as there were before the Holocaust.

By 1980 the estimated rate of Jewish intermarriage in some areas of the United States was as high as 40 percent. The Jewish proportion of the total U.S. population declined from 3.7 percent in 1937 to 2.9 percent in 1963 and only about 2.4 percent in 1985. If present trends continue, it is estimated that by the year 2000 no more than 1.6 percent of the American population will be Jewish. A rising rate of intermarriage is undoubtedly a major cause of this proportional

During the Holocaust, more than one-third of the world's Jewish population perished.

In the wake of the Holocaust, how do assimilation and intermarriage threaten Jewish survival?

population decline, since the vast majority of children born of mixed marriages are lost to the Jewish people and Judaism. As Rabbi David Einhorn, one of the early leaders of American Reform Judaism, wrote nearly a century ago: "Intermarriage drives a nail in the coffin of Judaism."

Concern over Jewish survival helps explain the apparent inconsistency between the books of Ezra and Ruth. When Ezra issued his decree against mixed marriages, the Jewish people had just returned from exile in Babylon. Their Jewish loyalties had been weakened by the fact that so many of them had already intermarried with the Babylonians, and the children they brought back with them had neither knowledge of nor attachment to Jewish tradition. Ezra felt it necessary to ban intermarriage because he feared that, without such drastic action, his people's identity as Jews would be wholly obliterated.

Ruth's situation differed from Ezra's in three important respects. First, her decision was primarily personal, affecting her own religious loyalties and not the survival of an entire people. Second, the Jewish people in her time were not faced, as they were in the time of Ezra, by the threat of imminent extinction. Third, Ruth was a Jew-by-choice, who maintained her Jewish identity after her husband's death and who afterward married another Jew. What makes Ruth's example all the more impressive and important is the fact that Jewish tradition considers her to be an ancestor of King David—hence of the Messiah, who, it was believed, would descend from David.

Judaism and civilization

The second reason for Jewish opposition to intermarriage rests on the belief that Jews have made—and must continue to make—a distinctive contribution to humanity. Jews have compiled a record of accomplishment in virtually every category of human endeavor, as philosophers, political and business leaders, athletes, scientists, artists, writers, and musicians. Probably you can name many of these great Jewish men and women. In this case, however, our concern is less with individual achievements by people who happened to be Jews than with certain specifically Jewish gifts to the world.

More than any other people known to history, Jews have searched for the unifying principle that holds the universe together. This is the essence of what we mean by the Shema. "Hear, O Israel"— understand this, you who call yourselves Jews—"the Lord is our God, the Lord is one"—there is an essential unity, a cohesiveness, a oneness binding together the entire universe and all it contains. This unity embraces all the planets and galaxies, as well as all living creatures on our own planet.

This unity, which our ancestors were the first to discern, remains today a driving force in the world of science. Albert Einstein devoted the last years of his life to searching for one unified theory that would explain the underlying principles of physics. Charles Darwin, from a different perspective and with a different intent, established through his theory of evolution the essential unity of all life forms on this earth. Hear, O Israel!

Nor has the quest for unity been our only contribution. We Jews have also been collectively unique in applying the in-

sights of ethics to all areas of human life. From the beginning we have recognized our particular loyalty to our fellow Jews in our own communities and elsewhere, yet we have also understood that our Jewish ties are valid only if they lead us to concern for all peoples everywhere. Finally, despite an incomparable burden of suffering, we Jews have maintained an attitude of evolving optimism and hope. We continue to believe in the possibility of a messianic age, when no one will suffer the ravages of war, poverty, or disease.

Judaism's unique burden, mission, and opportunity were expressed in a parable by a famous preacher popularly known as "the Dubno":

The designation of Israel by God as His particular people can be compared, explains the Dubno, to a nobleman who desires to extract taxes from his many subjects. Since it is impossible for him to go to each individual person separately, he designates one or two appointees who take the responsibility of collection upon themselves. But while, in the end, all the subjects pay their imposed taxes, it is the special appointees alone from whom the nobleman demands the funds.

H. A. Glatt, He Spoke in Parables *(Jay Bithmar, 1957), p. 115*

Rabbi Eugene Borowitz has articulated much the same thought as follows:

There is no group whose record of continuing devotion to ethical excellence, whose moral persistence in the face of the most inhuman treatment and whose stamina in pursuit of the humane, is greater than that of the Jews. Any man whose concern for morality goes very deep ought to honor their achievement and, if he is without similar roots or an equivalent community to empower and fulfill his ethical striving, consider joining them. But if one is born a Jew, is already part of that group, has already in some way been shaped by their his-

toric continuity, he ought to recognize that the roots of his own ethical stubbornness almost entirely stem from his Jewishness.

Eugene Borowitz, The Mask Jews Wear *(Simon & Schuster, 1973), p. 96*

In the Dubno's parable, who is the nobleman? Who are the tax collectors? Are you comfortable with the way this parable portrays the relationship between the people of Israel and the other peoples of the world? If not, why not? How might you recast the Dubno's parable to express more accurately your own feelings about the relationship among God, the Jews, and the rest of humanity?

What do you think Borowitz means by "ethical stubbornness"? Do you think this trait is particularly Jewish? Do the Jews you know show "continuing devotion to ethical excellence"? If not, in what ways could they—and you—improve?

How would you assess the contributions of Jews, both individually and collectively, to scientific, ethical, and religious thought? Do you think the world would be very different today if the Jewish people had never existed? How can Jews today best live up to the ideals embodied in their cultural and religious heritage?

Some people say that Jews who intermarry and raise their children as Gentiles mock the memory of the six million Jews who died in the Holocaust. Do you agree? Do the sufferings of our martyrs during the Holocaust and other periods in Jewish history impose special responsibilities on all Jews today?

In a shop window, Jewish and Christian symbols appear side-by-side.

What role did Judaism play in the birth of Christianity? What distinctive contributions has Judaism made to the development of civilization worldwide?

Religion and marital happiness

The third reason for opposing intermarriage is that it lessens a couple's chances for happiness. All reliable studies indicate that the divorce rate among mixed-marriage couples is between three and four times higher than that of couples who share the same religion. In 1988 alone, there were more than 500,000 divorces among interfaith couples with children.

A constant debate over whether to celebrate Ḥanukkah or Christmas, Pesaḥ or Easter, Shabbat or Sunday, can and often does plague intermarried couples. Even if such couples vow to remain neutral —already a damaging disservice to their children, who are thereby deprived of the spiritual security and enrichment they need—grandparents on both sides are likely to create tension. Just as a shared religious experience can strongly contribute to marital happiness, so religious differences can have a powerfully destructive effect.

Have you or any of your friends grown up in a mixed-marriage household? To what extent did religious differences intrude on family happiness? How did the parents resolve the question of which holidays they should celebrate? Where they should worship? Which religious school their children should attend?

To what extent might the warnings about mixed marriages apply equally to Jewish couples with different degrees of religious commitment? Suppose the wife wants to keep a kosher home and attend religious services regularly, while the husband has little interest in synagogue or dietary laws. In what ways would their situation be similar to that of an intermarried couple? How would it be different?

Whether to celebrate Ḥanukkah or Christmas— or both—is just one of many conflicts a mixed-marriage couple must cope with. What is the best way to ensure that the children receive a Jewish upbringing?

A run for Soviet Jewry.

Israel Solidarity Day in
Los Angeles.

**To what extent will children
born of mixed marriages be
willing to support Jewish
causes?**

Should a rabbi agree to perform a mixed marriage? To what extent should the rabbi warn the couple about the obstacles their marriage may face? What assurances, if any, should the rabbi require concerning how the couple plans to resolve their religious differences? Which rituals the couple will observe? How their children will be raised?

Jews-by-choice

Virtually all Jewish authorities today agree that if a Jew and a non-Jew are determined to marry, the Gentile partner should become a Jew-by-choice. Assuming that the conversion is sincere and the couple then lives an active Jewish life, the probability of Jewish survival is obviously increased. Differences in background and culture cannot be obliterated by conversion, but the likelihood of marital conflict will certainly be reduced.

In each of the following sets of alternatives, which is preferable? Which factors influenced your decision?

1a. A marriage between a Jew and a white Christian who is not willing to become Jewish.

1b. A marriage between a Jew and a black Christian who is willing to become Jewish.

2a. An unhappy marriage between two Jews.

2b. A happy marriage between a Jew and a Gentile.

3a. A Jew marries a Gentile who becomes a Jew-by-choice. They practice many Jewish rituals in their home, join a synagogue, and send their children to Hebrew school.

3b. A Jew marries a Jew. They neither practice Jewish rituals at home nor belong to a synagogue nor enroll their children in any kind of Jewish school.

Motives, responses, responsibilities

As with most emotion-laden decisions in life, the underlying causes of mixed dating and mixed marriage can be highly complex. The choice of a non-Jewish marriage partner may represent an unconscious desire to strike out against the parent, especially if the parent has vehemently opposed intermarriage. Such a choice may also betray feelings of discomfort or discontent with being Jewish.

On the other hand, some mixed marriages take place for no reason more subtle than the fact that two people of different faiths have fallen in love.

On the parents' side, opposition to a mixed marriage can go far beyond reasonable and tolerable limits. Some parents even go to the inexcusable extreme of sitting shivah for a son or daughter who marries a non-Jew, treating the child as if he or she were dead. Sometimes the parents who react most extremely are those who have been least observant of Jewish tradition and ritual. Perhaps it's their own negligence or failure which they unconsciously resent in their child.

Whatever the motives for intermarriage, the Jewish partner and his or her parents have the responsibility to do everything they can (a) to enhance the probability of Jewish survival, (b) to increase the couple's chances for marital happiness, and (c) to foster harmony and love within and between the families involved.

Men and Women

CHAPTER ELEVEN

MEN, WOMEN, SEX

Clark Gable and Vivien Leigh in *Gone With the Wind* (1939).

Do you ever have fantasies about sharing a moment of passion with someone you love?

Time of transition

This is an exciting and stimulating time in your life. If its challenges and opportunities haven't moved you yet, they soon will.

The choice of college and career, the search for your own personal identity, the tension caused by the transition from childhood to adult responsibilities —these are among the stresses, strains, and joys of adolescence. Greater than any of these, however—indeed, under-lying and motivating many of them—is the emergence of your full sexuality. Bodily juices are flowing now within you more profusely than ever before. Urges and desires you felt only occasion-ally in earlier years now press them-selves upon you with increasing frequency and power. The ways in which you learn to develop and fulfill your sexuality now and in these next few years will affect the rest of your life most profoundly.

Christianity and sex

Generally speaking, early Christian thinkers were extremely negative and suspicious in their attitude toward sex. Unlike nearly all the principal figures of the Hebrew Bible and the Talmud, Jesus never married. In order to remove Jesus from any taint of sex, Christians fostered the belief that he was born to a virgin. St. Paul, who was the real founder of Christianity, and who also never married, looked upon sexual desire and especially sexual intercourse as evil. He thought of marriage merely as a concession to human weakness:

It is well for a man not to touch a woman. But because of the temptation to immorality, each man should have his own wife and each woman her own husband. . . .

To the unmarried and the widows I say that it is well for them to remain single as I do. But if they cannot exercise self-control, they should marry. For it is better to marry than to be aflame with passion.

I Corinthians 7:1-9

This distrust of sex is echoed in the views of the other church fathers:

He who loves his wife too ardently is an adulterer.

St. Jerome

The only legitimate purpose of sexual intercourse, said the church, was to produce children:

Intercourse even with one's legitimate wife is unlawful and wicked where the conception of offspring is prevented.

St. Augustine

Although some Protestant groups take a more liberal view of human sexuality, the belief that sex is wrong if not directed at producing children remains a strong current in Roman Catholic teaching.

Have you ever discussed with your Christian friends topics such as birth control, abortion, and homosexuality? How do their church teachings about sex differ from what you've learned at home and in religious school? To what extent have your friends been influenced by what they've been taught in church? Are your own views similar to those of your parents and teachers, or do your current beliefs differ significantly from what you've been taught in the past?

How is human sexuality like that of animals? How does it differ?

Discussing birth control pills at a family planning clinic.

A holy thing?
An evil impulse?

We find in some Jewish authorities the same distrust of sex the early Christians felt:

We ought to limit sexual intercourse altogether, hold it in contempt, and desire it only rarely. . . . The act is too base to be performed except when needed.

Maimonides, Guide for the Perplexed, *3:49*

But a Hebrew marriage manual written during the thirteenth century boldly challenged Maimonides' view:

Intercourse is a holy and pure thing when it is done in an appropriate way, in an appropriate time, and with an appropriate intention. Let no man think

that in proper intercourse there is anything blameworthy or perverse. Heaven forfend, for intercourse is called "knowing" . . . and if it were not a matter of great holiness it would not have been called that. The matter certainly is not as Maimonides thought, as described in the *Guide for the Perplexed*, where he praises Aristotle for saying that the sense of touch is a shame to men. Heaven defend us from such errors. . . . But we, the children of the masters of the holy Torah, believe that God created all things according to the wisdom of His will . . . and if our sexual organs are a disgrace, how could it happen that God created a thing which was blemished, shameful, or faulty?

Iggeret Hakodesh, *chap. 2*

What might the author of *Iggeret Hakodesh* have meant by "in an appropriate way, in an appropriate time, and with an appropriate intention"? Are expressions of sexual intimacy appro-

How do Judaism and Roman Catholicism differ in their teachings about birth control?

priate at all times and places? Are they appropriate at religious services? In the classroom? On the job? On a public street? When one partner is feeling ill? After one partner has asked the other to stop?

Undoubtedly you know that in Orthodox synagogues men and women are not permitted to sit together; women must worship in the balcony or, if there is no balcony, in a separate section. This, incidentally, was also true in many churches during the early history of Christianity. What do you think was (and is) the main reason for this separation? Do you agree? Does this separation of the sexes discriminate against women? What does it say about men?

Two rabbinic passages emphasize the importance of sexuality and of restraint:

[The Israelites] said, "Since this is a time of grace for us, let us pray that the Evil Impulse be handed over to us." They prayed and he was given to them. But the prophet Elijah warned them: "Understand that if you kill the Evil Impulse, the whole world will collapse."

Nevertheless, they imprisoned the Evil Impulse for three days. But when they looked for a fresh egg, none could be found in all the land of Israel.

"What shall we do?" the people asked each other. "Shall we kill him? But without the Evil Impulse, the world cannot survive...." So they put out his eyes and let him go.

Yoma 69b

Were it not for the Evil Impulse, no man would build a house, marry a wife, or beget children.

Genesis Rabbah 9:7

What did the rabbis mean by the term "Evil Impulse"? Do you believe the use of such terms helps or hinders mature discussion of human sexuality? Why did fresh eggs disappear when the Evil Impulse was imprisoned? What would happen if the Evil Impulse were killed altogether? How do you evaluate the ending of the parable from Yoma?

Sex as a mitzvah

Is sex mainly for the purpose of creating new life? Or is sex one of life's pleasures that both men and women have not only the opportunity but also the responsibility to enjoy? Jewish tradition offers the following prayer for a husband to recite before having intercourse with his wife:

O, Lord my God and God of my fathers, ground of all the universe . . . may it be Your will that You emanate from Your spirit of power unto me and give me might and strength in my organs and my body that I might regularly fulfill the commandment pertaining to my sexual cycle; that there not be found in my organs, body or passion any weakness or slackness; that there be no forcing, unseemly thought, confusion of mind, or weakening of power to prevent me from fulfilling my desire with my wife. Rather, now and forever, let my passion be ready for me without fail or slackness of organ, at any time that I should desire. Amen.

Sefer Likutei Tzevi, p. 126

Whose sexual needs are of primary importance in this prayer—the husband's, his wife's, or those of both partners? Could you recast this prayer into one a wife might say before having sex with her husband? Into one that both husband and wife could say together?

Sex in marriage is a *mitzvah* in and of itself, independent of the imperative of *p'ru ur'vu* ("be fertile and increase"—Genesis 1:28). This is the *mitzvah* of conjugal rights, owed by a husband to his wife; it must be placed on the scale alongside the procreational duty. The source is Exodus 21:10, where we are told that if a man takes a wife, he must provide her with three goods in return for her having become his wife. He must provide her with food, shelter and conjugal rights. The conjugal rights are of a given frequency, whether or not procreation is now or ever possible....

And, lest the husband feel he can absolve himself with a token fulfillment of this pledge, the Mishnah sets forth a recommended frequency, based on the husband's health, age and occupation. If he now wants to change his occupation from what it was before marriage—from one that allowed him to remain home more to one which requires him to be away from home more often—the Talmud says he may not make this occupational change without his wife's permission. With the *mitzvah* of marital sex involved, he cannot make a unilateral decision in this matter.

David K. Feldman, Health and Medicine in the Jewish Tradition *(Crossroad, 1986), pp. 56f*

According to Feldman, whose sexual needs are of primary importance in marriage—the husband's, his wife's, or those of both partners? What implications do you draw from the idea that sex is a *mitzvah*? How does this attitude toward sexuality differ from St. Augustine's insistence that marital sex "is unlawful and wicked where the conception of offspring is prevented"? How does it differ from the rabbis' depiction of sex as the "Evil Impulse"?

Do you approve of the idea that a husband should not change his job without his wife's permission? Do you think Feldman would agree that a wife may not change her job without her husband's permission? In general, do you think the principle that a husband and wife should secure each other's approval before making major changes in their lives is a prescription for a healthy marriage? What problems does it raise? What problems does it avoid?

Birth control

Because Judaism and Roman Catholicism differ in their views of human sexuality, they also diverge in their attitudes toward birth control, or contraception. The only form of birth control approved by the Roman Catholic Church is the rhythm method, which the church calls natural contraception. All other methods, which the church calls artificial, are prohibited.

Because a woman can become pregnant only during certain days of her menstrual cycle, in theory it is possible to avoid having children by limiting intercourse to the days when she is unable to conceive. The trouble is that determining which days these are and limiting intercourse accordingly is anything but exact. A couple can produce quite a sizable family while experimenting to discover their own personal rhythm.

Judaism rejects the distinction between natural and artificial methods of birth control. For us, wearing a condom or inserting a diaphragm is no more artificial than making use of any other modern medical technique. On five separate occasions the Talmud not only approves birth control but even suggests what was then considered to be a reliable method:

There are three women who, when experiencing sex relations with their husbands, may [or must?] take the precaution of using an absorbent to prevent conception: a minor, a pregnant woman, and a woman who is still nursing her baby.

Yevamot 12b, 100b; Ketubot 39a; Niddah 45a; Nedarim 35b

How can we explain the differing views of Judaism and Roman Catholicism on birth control? Does the encouragement of sexual intercourse for married couples cheapen or enrich the value of sex in their lives? Why?

Why do Orthodox synagogues seat men and women in different sections?

"Pro-life" and "pro-choice" demonstrators mark the anniversary of the Supreme Court decision that legalized abortion in the United States.

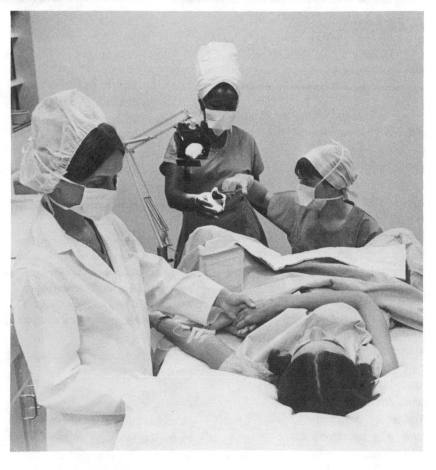

What restrictions, if any, do you think should be placed on abortion? Is abortion acceptable as a routine method of birth control?

Inside an abortion clinic.

Abortion

The Roman Catholic Church and certain Protestant groups argue that the deliberate termination of pregnancy is murder because, in their tradition, a fetus is considered to be a human being from the instant of conception. The Jewish tradition, on the other hand, thinks of the fetus not as a human being but as an appendage of the mother's body.

While Judaism does not favor abortion for frivolous reasons or as a form of birth control, it does approve abortion under certain circumstances, especially when the mother's life is at stake. Most Reform and many Conservative or Reconstructionist rabbis would also permit abortion if continuation of the pregnancy seriously threatened the woman's emotional or mental health; even many Orthodox rabbis would allow abortion if carrying the fetus to term might drive an expectant mother to either hysteria or suicide. Most non-Orthodox rabbis today permit abortion when the pregnancy resulted from incest or rape, or where there is reason to fear that the child may be born seriously defective.

Do you think women should have absolute freedom to choose for themselves whether they wish to have an abortion? If not, what restrictions on abortion would you impose? Would you allow abortion if the woman's physical health is in danger? If her mental or emotional health is threatened? When the pregnancy resulted from rape or incest? If the child is likely to be seriously defective? If the fetus is already seven months old?

In disputed cases, who should decide when an abortion should be permitted? The woman's doctor? A panel of religious experts? Local courts? The federal government? Should the husband, boyfriend, or parents have the right to be notified before an abortion is performed? Should they have to right to intervene to prevent the procedure from taking place? If abortion is outlawed, should doctors who perform abortions be treated as criminals and sent to jail? Should women who have abortions also be prosecuted and punished?

Masturbation

By the time they reach adulthood, virtually 100 percent of males and about 60 percent of females have masturbated. Until recently, masturbation was frowned on by both medical and religious authorities. In Judaism it was referred to as "adultery by the hand."

The tradition has considered masturbation as a sin and has strictly prohibited it. Any seed which was brought forth in vain involved a sin which was punishable by God. . . . This prohibition was carried even further, and anyone who excessively touched his genitals was considered a transgressor. . . .

There is no mention in the Talmudic literature about women masturbating. The only reference to it is a folk saying: "He masturbates with a pumpkin and his wife with a cucumber." Of course, these practices are vigorously rejected. . . .

The matter was taken up again in connection with the question of artificial insemination. The sperm must be obtained through masturbation or through withdrawal before completing intercourse. Orthodox authorities are divided on whether this is permitted under these special circumstances. Those who are permissive have felt that in this case the sperm is not being wasted, while the opponents reject this interpretation. . . .

Although the statements of tradition are very clear, we would take a different view of masturbation, in the light of current psychological thought.

Rabbi Walter Jacob, American Reform Responsa *(CCAR, 1983), pp. 479f*

The question of masturbation is one of many matters on which liberal Jews must respect our tradition without necessarily following it. We cannot limit ourselves to the insights of our ancestors regarding masturbation because our knowledge on this question greatly exceeds theirs. Medical and psychiatric experts today are virtually unanimous in agreeing that masturbation is not harmful and does not cause any of the disasters once attributed to it. The only harm resulting from masturbation is the profound but unwarranted sense of guilt resulting from the stern warnings against it in the past.

Pornographic movies and books are commonly called "adult." Do they really reflect an adult view of sexuality? What important aspects of sexuality do they leave out?

Pornography

The dictionary defines *pornography* as "obscene literature or art." The word comes from two Greek terms meaning "prostitute" and "writing." For practical purposes, we can define pornography as the deliberate use of obscene photographs, films, or descriptions for the express purpose of stimulating sexual desire.

What's wrong with that? Two things. First, it encourages one person to anticipate using another for his or her selfish gratification. Second, it reduces sex to a purely physical experience. In ways I shall try to clarify in the next chapter, to be fully human, sexual intercourse should express and reinvigorate both the physical and the spiritual aspects of love. Pornography can't possibly address the spiritual side of sexuality. Pornography cheapens what should be sacred.

Does that mean that from a Jewish point of view you commit a sin if you "read" *Playboy* or *Playgirl*? No, not at all. Not even if you masturbate while fantasizing with such photographs. The danger comes only if you limit your sexual interest permanently to that level, if you fail to develop a more mature appreciation of love and sexuality, involving both physical and spiritual bonds between you and your partner.

You shall not make yourself a sculptured image, or any likeness of what is in the heavens above, or on the earth below, or in the waters under the earth. You shall not bow down to them or serve them.

Exodus 20:4-5

Some Jewish authorities interpret this Second Commandment to apply to pornography as well as idolatry. In what ways do pornography and idolatry resemble each other? Are there any significant differences? Do you believe that constant exposure to pornography has a harmful effect on people?

Some American towns and cities have tried to restrict or ban outright the sale of pornographic materials. Do you agree with their approach? If so, what kinds of materials would you restrict? How would you restrict them? Would you apply special restrictions on the use of young children in pornography? On the depiction of violence against women or men? On photographs showing homosexual acts?

Depending on language, violence, and sexual content, movies are classified *G*, *PG*, *PG-13*, *R*, and *X*, and in some cases access to them is restricted by age. Do you favor such restrictions? If so, do you think such a classification system should be extended to magazines? Books? Records and tapes? How would you answer the objections of those who contend that all such restrictions limit artistic creativity and violate our First Amendment rights of free expression?

Homosexuality

Far from being a new or modern phenomenon, homosexuality was well known in ancient and medieval times.

The two angels arrived in Sodom in the evening, as Lot was sitting in the gate of Sodom. When Lot saw them, he rose to greet them and, bowing low with his face to the ground, he said, "Please, my lords, turn aside to your servant's house to spend the night. . . ."

They had not yet lain down when the townspeople, the men of Sodom . . . surrounded the house. And they shouted to Lot and said to him, "Where are the men who came to you tonight? Bring them out to us, that we may be intimate with them." So Lot went out to them at the entrance, shut the door behind him, and said, "I beg you, my friends, do not commit such a wrong. See, I have two daughters who have not known a man. Let me bring them out to you, and you may do to them as you please; but do

not do anything to these men, since they have come under the shelter of my roof." But they said, "Stand back!" . . . And they pressed hard against the person of Lot, and moved forward to break the door. But the men stretched out their hands and pulled Lot into the house with them, and shut the door. . . .

Then the men said to Lot, "Whom else have you here? Sons-in-law, your sons and daughters, or anyone else you have

Are these men homosexuals? You can't really tell from a photo. But would you feel any differently about them if you knew for sure they were?

113

Should homosexuals be encouraged to join predominantly heterosexual congregations? Or should new congregations be organized especially to provide for homosexuals' spiritual needs?

in the city—bring them out of the place. For we are about to destroy this place; because the outcry against them before the Lord has become so great that the Lord has sent us to destroy it."

Genesis 19:1-13

Were you surprised by what the men of Sodom asked Lot to do? Were you shocked at Lot's response? Why do you think Lot responded as he did? What does his response show about the status of women in the biblical world? About the obligations owed to a guest? If Lot's visitors had been homosexuals and had been willing to let the men of Sodom do what they wanted, would the Sodomites still have deserved to be punished? Why or why not?

We have explicit and direct evidence that the Bible and later Jewish tradition considered homosexuality sinful:

If a man lies with a male as one lies with a woman, the two of them have done an abhorrent thing; they shall be put to death—their bloodguilt is upon them.

Leviticus 20:13

A woman must not put on man's apparel, not shall a man wear woman's clothing; for whoever does these things is abhorrent to the Lord your God.

Deuteronomy 22:5

Some writers have cited this passage from Deuteronomy in arguing against "unisex" fashions and hairstyles. Do you think this is what the author of the passage had in mind? If so, to what extent should we be guided by such a biblical prohibition?

Women are forbidden to engage in lesbian practices with one another, these being "the doings of the land of Egypt" against which we have been warned. . . .

A man should be particularly strict with his wife in this matter, and should prevent women known to indulge in such practices from visiting her, and her from going to visit them.

Maimonides, Code, *"Laws Concerning Forbidden Intercourse," 21:8*

In this section of his *Code*, how does Maimonides portray the relationship between husband and wife? Do you believe either marriage partner should have the right to restrict the other's friendships? If so, when? Does it make a difference whether the friend is male or female?

Modern views

Without exception, all those whose views are recorded in the Bible and Talmud condemn homosexuality. In our time, however, some rabbinic voices have dissented. One of them is Janet Marder, rabbi of a mostly gay and lesbian congregation in California.

And so I had to decide: how much did it matter to me that the voice of my tradition, without exception, ran counter to the evidence of my experience and the deepest promptings of my conscience?

For me the choice was clear. I could not be guided by laws which seem profoundly unjust and immoral. I believe, and I teach my congregants, that Jewish law condemns their way of life. But I teach also that I cannot accept that law as authoritative. It belongs to me, it is part of my history, but it has no binding claim on me. In my view, the Jewish consideration of homosexuality is the work of human beings—limited, imperfect, fearful of what is different, and, above all, concerned with ensuring tribal survival. In short, I think our ancestors were wrong about a number of things, and homosexuality is one of them.

The Reconstructionist *(October / November 1985), p. 23*

Rabbi Marder is not homosexual; she is married and the mother of a child. Would her opinion be more or less valid if she herself were a lesbian? Is her approach likely to increase the number of Jewish homosexuals? Why or why not? What effect might her statement have on those who are already lesbians or gays? Should we encourage or discourage the establishment of congregations especially dedicated to providing for homosexuals' spiritual needs?

Equally interesting is the opinion of Eugene Mihaly, Professor of Rabbinic Literature at the Hebrew Union College-Jewish Institute of Religion. Dr. Mihaly was first ordained an Orthodox rabbi, then a second time as a Reform rabbi.

[W]e know today that in the overwhelming number of cases, the homosexual is not a willful, volitional rebel. He is either that way from birth or became a homosexual in early childhood or adolescence. In any case, that is the way he is. At the very least, therefore, he would, even according to traditional *halakha*, in the light of our present knowledge, have to be treated as . . . one who acts under duress and merits all the sympathy, consideration, kindness that the *halakha* extends to the victim, the one who is forced to act under duress.

E. Mihaly, Responsum on Homosexuality, *p. 19*

These two quotations from Rabbis Marder and Mihaly once again raise questions we must wrestle with constantly in seeking to develop an authentic modern Jewish ethic. How do we decide when to reject, when to accept, and when to modify traditional Jewish teaching? Who is qualified to make such decisions? How would questions like these be answered differently by Orthodox, Conservative, Reconstructionist, and Reform Jews? Could Dr. Mihaly have remained an Orthodox rabbi with his current opinion on homosexuality?

Gay congregations? Lesbian rabbis?

Several congregations catering especially to the religious needs of homosexuals have already been admitted to the Union of American Hebrew Congregations. Reform authorities continue to disagree on whether the UAHC was justified in accepting such groups.

Homosexuality is deemed in Jewish tradition to be a sin. . . . Nevertheless, it would be in direct contradiction to Jewish law to keep sinners out of the congregation. To isolate them into a

Does your community make homosexuality a crime? Or does it have laws protecting homosexuals from discrimination?

separate congregation and thus increase their mutual availability is certainly wrong.

Solomon B. Freehof, in W. Jacobs (ed.), American Reform Responsa *(CCAR, 1973), p. 51*

In principle, such a synagogue should not exist, because all synagogues should be so open that all Jews may feel fully welcome and at home in them. But clearly, that is not the way our world or our family-oriented congregations are constituted today. Until temples are able to accept Jewish homosexuals *in their homosexuality* . . . homosexuals who want their own congregations should not only be allowed to have them but encouraged and assisted and accorded full membership in the Union of American Hebrew Congregations.

Sanford Ragins, "An Echo of the Pleas of Our Fathers," CCAR Journal *(Summer 1973), p. 46*

Some have now questioned the need for synagogues whose membership is primarily gay and lesbian. Members of these synagogues reply that they, too, hope the time will come when such congregations are no longer needed. They feel the need will end when gay people are welcomed—not just tolerated—in the mainstream congregations; when two women can be called to the Torah to celebrate their twenty years together as lovers; when two men can bring the infant daughter they have adopted to the synagogue to be named, blessed and welcomed into the household of Israel.

Robert M. Rankin, "Homosexuality: The New Understanding," in Keeping Posted, *vol. 32, no. 2, p. P10.*

The CCAR Responsa Committee has answered this question negatively. Based on the assumption that Jewish community

leaders should exemplify "the highest personal and moral qualities" and that their conduct must be "above reproach," the committee has ruled:

Overt heterosexual behavior or overt homosexual behavior which is considered objectionable by the community disqualifies the person involved from leadership positions in the Jewish community. We reject this type of individual as a role model within the Jewish community.

S. B. Freehof in American Reform Responsa, *p. 54*

Do you agree with this answer? Why or why not? Does the opening statement treat heterosexuals and homosexuals equally? Should it? Can a homosexual possess "the highest personal and moral qualities"? Would *every* heterosexual be a better role model for children than *any* homosexual? Does the CCAR decision rule out all homosexuals or only those who have "come out of the closet"?

Trying to understand

In concluding this chapter, let me offer my own personal testimony:

Many years ago, teaching a high school course on marriage, I asked my students to help me define love. We finally came up with something like this: love is a physical and spiritual relationship between two persons that enables each to achieve a greater potential than either could attain alone. At that point a perceptive student asked whether this could apply to a homosexual couple. My immediate and emphatic response was no. Later I apologized to the class. Reflection convinced me that our definition could indeed encompass two men or two women who loved each other physically and spiritually.

This does not mean that I equate homosexual and heterosexual love. At least for the foreseeable future, gay or lesbian couples risk public opprobrium. They are also vulnerable to such social exploitation as blackmail and job discrimination. Even more importantly, they generally are deprived of love's more enriching fulfillment, creating a family of their own.

Responsum by R. Gittelsohn in Keeping Posted, *vol. 32, no. 1*

People your age often have two types of fear regarding homosexuality. The first fear you may feel, on occasion, is that you yourself may be lesbian or gay. Experts agree that just having a crush on someone of the same sex doesn't make you a homosexual; most teenagers who go through this quite common stage emerge as heterosexuals. The second fear is that a homosexual may approach you and solicit you as a potential partner. The truth is that if you reject such an advance tactfully but firmly, it is extremely unlikely to be repeated.

How comfortable would you feel having an acknowledged homosexual as your rabbi, cantor, or teacher? Does your community have a congregation that caters especially to the spiritual needs of lesbians and gays? Does your temple have any program to make homosexuals feel fully accepted and welcome? Does your rabbi counsel homosexuals to seek treatment and try to change their sexual orientation or to accept themselves as they are?

Does your community have any laws forbidding discrimination in employment and housing on the basis of "sexual preference"? If not, do you favor the passage of a gay rights law? What arguments have been used for and against such legislation?

CHAPTER TWELVE

IF NOT NOW, WHEN?

Every society in history has had rules about sex. Do you think our society's attitude toward premarital sex is too lenient? Too strict? Reasonable and proper?

Premarital sex

In Chapter Eleven we discussed, in general terms, the divergent attitudes of Judaism and Christianity toward sex. We also considered some of the ethical questions raised by birth control, abortion, masturbation, pornography, and homosexuality. One subject we did not discuss is important enough to merit special consideration: the question of premarital sexual intercourse.

You may be surprised to hear that early Jewish literature says little about the topic. The reason is that in ancient times couples were frequently betrothed in their early teens and usually married only a few years afterward. However, as the centuries passed and the gap between sexual maturation and the marriage age widened, Jewish authorities could not fail to address the problem. What they said about premarital intercourse was unequivocally negative:

Chastity before marriage has been considered an obvious requirement for all and was taken for granted by the tradition. . . . There are many statements which support this point of view and demand that an unmarried person refrain from sexual intercourse. The references deal particularly with males.

. . . A statement of Rabbi Yochanan makes this very clear: "There is a small organ in man; he who satisfies it goes hungry and he who allows it to go hungry is satisfied" (Sanhedrin 107a). . . .

All females were expected to be virgins at the time of their first marriage. The dowry of a non-virgin was less than that of a virgin, and anyone falsely claiming virginity was subject to severe punishment.

CCAR Committee on Responsa, American Reform Responsa *(CCAR, 1983), p. 477*

How might Rabbi Yochanan's statement be expressed in more modern terms? Is his opinion still valid? Does the selection offer any ethical reasons for remaining a virgin? How would you characterize the evidence the passage does offer? On what basis did Jewish communal authorities assume the right to punish false claims of virginity? Were they correct in doing so?

Desire and restraint

In few areas are we likely to find greater disagreement than on the question of premarital intercourse. At the same time, in few areas will we encounter a greater inclination to act by instinct or impulse instead of sound judgment. This is because the sex drive is one of the strongest forces in nature. You have probably already begun to feel its pressure inside yourself.

Like any powerful force, sex can yield either disastrous evil or incomparable good. This is why every society in history, everywhere and at all times, has developed rules to govern the sexual behavior of its citizens. Some of these rules have been too harsh, some too lenient. But a society that left all its members totally free to satisfy their sexual impulses would be courting disaster.

You are the only person in the world who can choose the basic direction of your own sex life. You are also the one who will benefit or suffer most because of that choice. If your sexuality expresses itself only as a search for physical stimulation, then you will experience sex but not sexual fulfillment. If, on the other hand, your sexuality is enriched by love and understanding, then you will experience not only physical pleasure in sex but also the deep satisfaction that only a spiritual and emotional commitment can bring.

Two modern Jewish experts have emphasized the emptiness of sex without love:

Because sexual desire is in the minds of most people coupled with the idea of love, they are easily misled to conclude that they love each other when they want each other physically. . . . If the desire for physical union is not stimulated by love, if erotic love is not also

Where have you learned most about sex? From your parents? From your teachers? From books? From swapping stories with your friends?

brotherly love, it never leads to union in more than an orgiastic, transitory sense. Sexual attraction creates, for the moment, the illusion of union, yet without love this "union" leaves strangers as far apart as they were before—sometimes it makes them ashamed of each other, because when the illusion has gone they feel their estrangement even more markedly than before. . . .

Love is not the result of adequate sexual satisfaction, but sexual happiness —even the knowledge of so-called sexual technique—is the result of love.

Erich Fromm, The Art of Loving *(Harper, 1956), pp. 54ff, 88ff*

What do you think Fromm means by emphasizing the need for "brotherly love" as well as "erotic love"? From his last paragraph, do you think Fromm would approve or disapprove of most sex manuals? Why?

I think highly of friendship, but sexual intercourse seems to me a rather extravagant way in which to express it. One should think so much of self, and what his most intimate giving of self means, that he should not do so without the most worthwhile reason. Or, to put it more positively, I value intercourse too highly as an inter-human experience for me to find it an appropriate act with a person who is only a friend.

E. Borowitz, Choosing a Sex Ethic *(Schocken, 1969), p. 107*

What do you think Rabbi Borowitz means when he writes that sex is "a rather extravagant way" of expressing friendship? What else should sexual intercourse express? Do you think Borowitz would argue that your husband or wife can't also be your friend?

Did Potiphar's wife really love Joseph? How do we know?

Facts of life

"All this is fine in principle," you may be thinking, "but the fact is that more and more young men and women are having intercourse before getting married, and an increasing number of unmarried couples are setting up households together. What should I say if my partner is pressuring me to go farther and faster than I really want to go?"

Here are two answers a young woman might give a man who says if she really loved him, she would go to bed with him:

1. "If you really love me, you won't ask me to do anything I find objectionable or distasteful."

2. "If your love for me depends on my satisfying your every need, you're not really in love with me. You're just confusing love with physical attraction."

How effective do you find these answers? Can you think of an answer that might

be even more effective? Would either of these two answers work for a young man who felt he wasn't ready for sex but was being pressured by his girlfriend?

When Joseph was taken down to Egypt, a certain Egyptian, Potiphar, a courtier of Pharaoh and his chief steward, bought him from the Ishmaelites. . . . [Potiphar] took a liking to Joseph. He made him his personal attendant and put him in charge of his household, placing in his hands all that he owned. . . . Now Joseph was well built and handsome.

After a time, his master's wife cast her eyes upon Joseph and said, "Lie with me." But he refused. He said to his master's wife, "Look, with me here, my master gives no thought to anything in this house, and all that he owns he has placed in my hands. He . . . has withheld nothing from me except yourself, since you are his wife. How then could I do this most wicked thing, and sin before God?" And much as she coaxed Joseph

What should you tell someone who is pressuring you to go farther and faster than you really want to go?

day after day, he did not yield to her request to lie beside her, to be with her.

One such day, he came into the house to do his work. None of the household being there inside, she caught hold of him by his coat and said, "Lie with me!" But he left his coat in her hand and got away and fled outside. . . . [S]he called out to her servants and said to them, "Look, he had to bring us a Hebrew to dally with us! This one came to lie with me; but I screamed loud. And when he heard me screaming at the top of my voice, he left his coat with me and got away and fled outside." She kept his coat beside her, until his master came home. Then she told him the same story. . . .

When his master heard the story that his wife told him . . . he was furious. So Joseph's master had him put in prison.

Genesis 39:1-20

Why did Joseph refuse to have intercourse with his master's wife? Was it because he was afraid of sex? Would he have been more of a man if he had yielded and gone to bed with her? Did Potiphar's wife really love Joseph? How do we know?

When no means no

Absalom son of David had a beautiful [half-]sister named Tamar, and Amnon son of David became infatuated with her. Amnon was so distraught because of his sister Tamar that he became sick; for she was a virgin, and it seemed impossible to Amnon to do anything to her. . . .

Amnon laid down and pretended to be sick. . . . Amnon said to the king, "Let my sister Tamar come and prepare a couple of cakes in front of me, and let her bring them to me. . . ." Tamar went to the house of her brother Amnon, who was in bed. She took dough and kneaded it into cakes in front of him, and cooked the cakes. . . . After everyone had withdrawn, Amnon said to

Tamar, "Bring the food inside and feed me." Tamar took the cakes she had made and brought them to her brother inside. But when she served them to him, he caught hold of her and said to her, "Come, lie with me, sister." But she said to him, "Don't, brother. Don't force me. Such things are not done in Israel! Don't do such a vile thing! . . ." But he would not listen to her; he overpowered her and lay with her by force.

Then Amnon felt a very great loathing for her; indeed, his loathing for her was greater than the passion he had felt for her. And Amnon said to her, "Get out!"

II Samuel 13:1-15

Of which serious crime was Amnon guilty? (The correct answer is *not* incest: in biblical times, marriage between a half-brother and half-sister was permitted.) Did Amnon really love Tamar? How do we know? Was Tamar responsible in any way for Amnon's actions? Was Amnon driven by a need for sex—or by a lust for power? How do you account for Amnon's sudden change in attitude after he forced himself on Tamar?

Does your community operate a rape crisis center? Are discussions of date rape available in the schools? What can people your age do to prevent date rape?

Cohabitation

While no precise figures are available, there has no doubt been a substantial increase in recent years of couples who decide to live together before marrying. Their usual claim is that cohabitation proves whether or not they are truly compatible, well enough matched to make marital success likely.

My experience as a counselor does not validate this claim. In my hundreds of counseling sessions with couples who have asked me to officiate at their weddings,

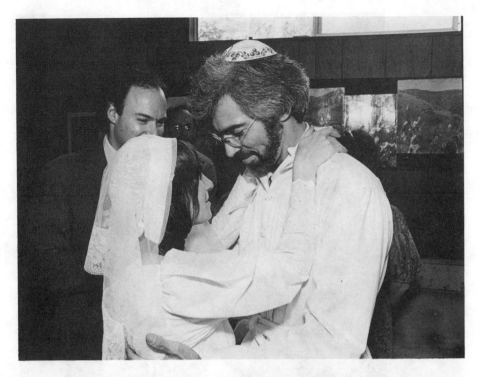

A Jewish wedding.

Is a marriage license "just a piece of paper"? Or does married life differ significantly from the relationship between a man and a woman who happen to be living and sleeping together?

A modern version of the traditional marriage contract, or ketubah.

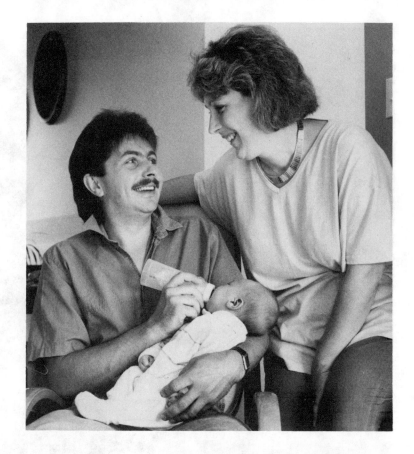

I have not found appreciably greater mutual understanding among those who have cohabited than among those who have not.

Even a sociologist who in general looks upon cohabitation favorably has admitted:

We must . . . remember that living together before marriage does not, according to recent research, mean greater chances of your marriage being successful. The divorce rate for couples who have lived together, sometimes for years, and then married, is as high as for those who did not live together.

This may be because they were immature, or it may mean there was some degree of commitment and/or responsibility which is withheld in the absence of a legal ceremony. Whichever the explanation, the result is that compatibility while living together unmarried is an unreliable test for living together successfully as a married couple.

Judith Fales, in R. Gittelsohn, Love, Sex, and Marriage *(UAHC, 1980), p. 210*

Some people who live together claim that marriage is a sham. "All it adds," they say, "is a contract, a piece of paper. If a man and a woman really love each other, that's all they need. We live together because of our love, not because we took part in a ceremony or signed a contract."

Are their contentions valid? Does the marriage ceremony, in and of itself, add anything significant to the relationship between husband and wife? Suppose the couple wants to have children. Do the marriage ceremony and license make a difference then?

Does sexual intercourse between two people who are married to each other differ in any important way from the same act involving the same individuals who are not married? Is intercourse between two persons who are married to each other always acceptable? Is intercourse between two persons who are not married to each other always unacceptable?

How do parenthood and family life enrich the marital relationship?

Male and female sexuality

Until relatively recent times it was commonly believed (or pretended?) that only men had strong sexual desires, derived great pleasure from intercourse, or should ever initiate a sexual encounter. Some traditional Jewish authorities, however, recognized a more active role for women in marital sex:

A woman who solicits her husband to the marital obligation will have children the like of whom did not exist even in the generation of Moses. . . .

Rabbi Isaac ben Avdimi said: "While a husband solicits with his speech, a wife solicits with her heart, this being a fine trait among women."

Eruvin 100b

A similar emphasis inheres in the popular Jewish superstition that if a wife experiences her orgasm before her husband has his, she will bear a son; if her husband's orgasm precedes hers, a daughter will be conceived. The importance of this belief—wrong as it was from a biological perspective—derives from the fact that sons were then preferred over daughters.

The recognition of women's sexual needs and pleasures has consequences not only in the relationship between husbands and wives but also in premarital experience. Several years ago a Harvard psychiatrist told me that increasingly among those who came to him on campus, the

female, not the male, was the sexual aggressor. Does this invalidate the opinion of Rabbi Isaac ben Avdimi?

In your own social world, do girls call boys on the telephone—or do they wait to be called? Do girls ask boys out on dates—or do they wait for the boys to do the asking? Do girls expect to share the costs of a date—or do they expect their food and entertainment to be paid for? In general, do you think dating customs and practices need to change? Or should they remain pretty much as they are?

AIDS

One phenomenon that has brought about a remarkable change in the way people think about sex in recent years is acquired immune deficiency syndrome, or AIDS.

AIDS cannot be caught through such ordinary contact as conversation or shaking hands. Nor can it be transmitted by drinking from the same glass or sitting on the same toilet seat. It is highly contagious, however, through sexual inter-

course, certain other sexual practices, blood transfusions using contaminated blood, or sharing a narcotics needle with a person who is infected. Although AIDS is more widespread among homosexuals than heterosexuals, it can be transmitted to heterosexuals in the several ways listed above.

Public health officials say that when you have sexual intercourse with someone, you are also having sex with everyone that person has had sex with over the last five years. Two people who have never had sexual intercourse with anyone else (and have not been exposed to AIDS in any other way) are not at risk of AIDS through intercourse. The greater the number of sex partners that either person has had previously, the greater the risk.

Despite intensive research, no effective treatment for AIDS has yet been discovered. In this respect, AIDS differs from such venereal diseases as syphilis or gonorrhea, which can also be transmitted through sexual intercourse. If diagnosed early enough, these infections can be arrested and cured; AIDS cannot.

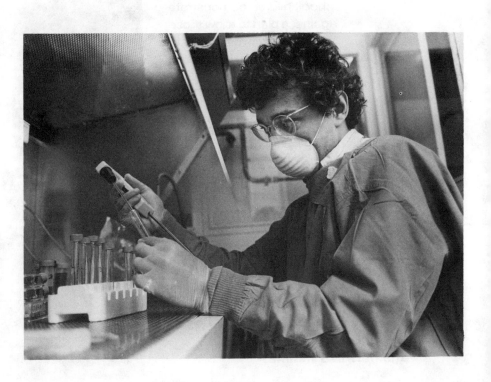

Searching for a cure for AIDS.

How has the threat of AIDS affected your attitude toward premarital and extramarital sex?

Thirteen-year-old Ryan White,
a hemophiliac who contracted
AIDS from contaminated
blood.

Schoolchildren demonstrate
against a plan to allow those
who test positive for AIDS to
attend normal classes.

**What can you do to help
prevent discrimination
against AIDS victims?**

Fears and fictions

Fear of contracting AIDS is perfectly justifiable. What is not justifiable is the prejudice that has been directed at AIDS victims because of ignorance and hysteria. Our sages were not immune to such prejudice:

Rabbi Jochanan says: "I go no closer to a leper than four cubits." Rabbi Simon says: "If the wind is blowing, I go no closer than a hundred cubits." Rabbi Ammi and Rabbi Assi say: "We do not even go near a place where lepers are known to live." Rabbi Eleazar ben Shimon was still afraid: If he heard that a leper was in the vicinity, he would hide. Then there was the great sage Resh Lakish. When he saw a leper, he would throw stones at him, shouting: "Stop contaminating us and go back to where you came from!"

Leviticus Rabbah 16:3

The first scare stories about AIDS provoked a similar response:

The AIDS epidemic has spawned a secondary scourge as deadly as the primary affliction: a wave of hysteria whose symptoms include ostracism, prejudice, and violence. AIDS victims, already serving a death sentence, are victimized a second time: they are tormented, thrown out of jobs, often spurned by family and friends; they have been denied admission to hospitals and refused desperately needed medical services; and organizations and even families offering refuge to patients have been subjected to bomb threats and vandalism.

Rabbi Alexander S. Schindler, Presidential Message, 58th General Assembly, UAHC, November 1985

Imagine a dialogue between Rabbi Schindler and the sages mentioned in Leviticus Rabbah. What might the sages have said to him? What might Schindler have answered? Suppose Schindler reminded the sages about the *mitzvah* of visiting the sick. What might they have responded? Does Judaism teach that we must risk our own health in order to help others? Which is worse: the ancients' shunning of lepers or the treatment of AIDS patients portrayed by Rabbi Schindler? Why? What can you do to protect yourself against AIDS? To encourage fairer treatment of its victims?

How can you reconcile the passage from Genesis Rabbah with the following story about Rabbi Akiba? Which represents the more authentically Jewish view?

It once happened that one of Rabbi Akiba's disciples became ill, and none of the sages visited him.

Then Rabbi Akiba himself went to the disciple's house, and because he saw to it that the floor was swept and sprinkled with water, the man recovered.

"My master, you have restored me to life," the disciple said.

Akiba went out and taught: "He who does not visit the sick is like someone who sheds blood."

Rabbi Dimi said: "He who visits the sick causes him to recover, and he who does not visit the sick causes him to die."

Nedarim 40a

Discrimination

It would be hard to exaggerate the amount of prejudice to which AIDS victims have been exposed. Many have lost their jobs or been expelled from their homes. In Florida three brothers who were infected by the AIDS virus through blood transfusions were expelled from school, and their home was set on fire. The family finally had to move out of the state.

Which of the following steps represent reasonable precautions against the spread of AIDS? Which represent unfair discrimination against AIDS victims? Explain in each case how you would protect the public against AIDS while protecting the rights of AIDS sufferers.

■ A newspaper columnist writes an article contending that AIDS is a punishment from God. He claims that AIDS victims deserve neither our sympathy nor our protection.

■ A student known to have AIDS registers at your school. A parents committee begins to gather petitions to have the student expelled. Some parents say they will refuse to allow their children to attend school as long as the AIDS victim continues to go there.

■ A local family-planning clinic advertises that it will distribute free condoms to anyone who asks. Contending that this step will encourage premarital sex, a group of parents and religious leaders demand that the clinic stop.

■ Some doctors in your community announce they will no longer treat AIDS victims because of the danger of contamination. They claim their other patients have expressed fear of catching the disease from AIDS patients.

■ A computer dating service requires that all its participants pass an AIDS screening test. Promising that all its members are AIDS-free, the service raises its membership fees.

■ The state legislature passes a law making it a felony for an AIDS victim to have sex without telling the partner or using a condom.

Condoms on display in a New York City drugstore.

How have the AIDS crisis and the rising tide of teen-age pregnancy changed public attitudes toward birth control? Do you think the greater openness about birth control will lead to an increase in premarital sex? If not, why not?

■ Local police move to close down bars and other hangouts where homosexuals and needle drug users gather.

■ The health department requires any doctor who treats someone with AIDS to notify the department about the case, so the department can track down and warn any of the AIDS victim's sex partners.

■ The health department also proposes to notify the AIDS victim's family, landlord, and school or employer.

■ A bill is submitted in the state legislature requiring all those diagnosed as having AIDS to be quarantined in special camps.

Protection

Only a few years ago the word "condom" never appeared in our daily newspapers and was seldom mentioned in polite conversation above a whisper. Now it is quite commonplace. This is largely because the use of a condom during sexual intercourse provides a reasonable (though by no means perfect) degree of protection against both AIDS and pregnancy. Do you think ads promoting condom use should be published? Will they encourage an increase in premarital sexual intercourse?

In the *Boston Globe* of May 17, 1987, appeared an article headlined "Many Teen-agers Disregard Danger." It reported that, according to a poll conducted by the Boston University School of Public Health, of some 600 Massachusetts teenagers who had experienced sexual intercourse, 54 percent said they were not concerned about AIDS and only 15 percent indicated that they had in any way changed their sexual behavior because of AIDS.

Ben Karlin, one of the students interviewed by the *Globe*, said to a reporter, "We're told that education is the best weapon, but some of our teachers seem to think that talking about AIDS will encourage us to go out and have sex."

Have your teachers shied away from discussing AIDS in the classroom? How comfortable are your teachers in discussing sex? How comfortable are you in talking about sexual matters with your teachers? Are you able to discuss such issues with your parents? If not, why not?

How can we explain the apparent indifference of so many high school students to the danger of AIDS? At what age do you think children should be told about AIDS? What has been the principal source of your sex education? Was it adequate? What do you wish had been included but was not?

Our experience with AIDS is still so recent that most answers must remain tentative. Among the conclusions that are already firm are the following:

1. Doctors, dentists, nurses, and medical technicians who come into contact with the blood and other bodily fluids of AIDS patients must wear rubber gloves, goggles, and other protective devices to guard themselves against infection.

2. Blood stored for transfusion must be carefully tested to make sure it is free from contamination.

3. Any person who knows or even suspects that he or she has been exposed to AIDS must also divulge this information to every potential sex partner and to all relevant medical personnel. Failure thus to disclose the potential danger is grossly and unforgivably immoral.

4. The terrible possibility of contracting AIDS must be factored into every decision whether to have sex. For the unmarried, the best protection against AIDS is to refrain from having premarital sexual intercourse. The next best protection against the sexual transmission of AIDS is to limit intercourse to a single partner, who, in turn, has had sex with no one else.

5. Where the slightest doubt exists regarding previous contact, the use of a condom should be imperative!

6. Except for realistic medical precautions, there must be no discrimination against AIDS patients and no infringement of their civil, political, or employment rights.

Your responsibility

You have two personal responsibilities regarding AIDS, both strongly recommended by traditional Jewish ethics:

First, to protect yourself in every reasonable way against infection by the AIDS virus;

Second, to help shape public opinion away from hysteria, and thus to safeguard the rights of those who are already infected. What, if anything, have you already done to meet these responsibilities? What, if anything, are you prepared to do from this point on?

Compare the following policies as protection against AIDS:

■ Wait until marriage to have sexual intercourse.

■ Limit your sexual activity to one partner who has never had intercourse with anyone else.

■ Make sure the male sex partner always wears a condom.

■ Limit your sexual activity to (a) friends you have known for a long time, (b) partners who have good reputations, or (c) people who look healthy.

On balance, which policies seem to offer the most protection? The least? Why?

Community

CHAPTER THIRTEEN

TAKING ADVANTAGE

Temptation

Paul didn't really take his school work seriously until the middle of his junior year. Until then, he did just enough to get barely passing grades and to remain eligible for varsity athletics. Suddenly he realized that with his mediocre average he would have trouble getting into a first-rate college. He began for the first time to exert himself. Although his grades improved significantly, they still weren't good enough to counterbalance his previous record.

As final exam time approached, Paul grew more and more apprehensive, especially about his weakest subject, social studies. Everything might well hinge on this one exam.

At that point, Paul's best friend, Milt, confided that he and another student, Larry, had searched their teacher's desk and found a copy of the exam questions. They offered to share them with Paul. Should he accept their proposal? Paul, Milt, and Larry had all applied to some of the same colleges, so declining their

Have you ever cheated on an exam? What would you do if you saw someone else cheating?

help might put Paul at a competitive disadvantage. Accepting would violate everything Paul had been taught about ethics and truth. What should he do?

Stealing, falsifying, excusing

You shall not steal; you shall not deal deceitfully or falsely with one another.

Leviticus 19:11

You shall not falsify measure of length, weight, or capacity. You shall have an honest balance, honest weights, an honest *ephah*, and an honest *hin*.

Leviticus 19:35f

This statement from Leviticus cautions specifically against cheating in business. What similarity, if any, do you see between cheating in business and cheating on an exam? Who is cheated when a merchant charges for a full pound of potatoes but the bag holds two ounces less? When a manufacturer calls a product apple juice that is mainly sugar water? When a used-car dealer alters the odometer to make a customer think a vehicle has been driven 20,000 miles instead of 120,000?

Rabbi [Menasheh] Klein observes that cheating involves two specific infractions of Jewish law. Such conduct . . . is akin to *genevat da'at*, a term which [can be] rendered as "misrepresentation." . . . Secondly, this type of misrepresentation may readily result in fraud in the fundamental sense of the term. Grades earned in courses serve to indicate proficiency

in the subject matter and to determine eligibility for scholarships. Moreover, it is assumed that an academic record reflects a level of competence which may be relied upon in determining whether the graduate is qualified to hold a position for which remuneration is paid. . . . An employer who, on the basis of grades earned, assumes that an employee has attained a level of competence which the employee has, in fact, not attained had been defrauded.**

J. David Bleich, Contemporary Halakhic Problems *(Yeshiva University Press, 1983), 2:110*

Who is cheated if Paul takes a test under false pretenses? Paul's teacher? His classmates? His school? The colleges to which he applies? In what sense might Paul be a victim of his own cheating?

What does a final exam "measure"? Who suffers if that measure turns out to be false?

Hillel used to say: If I am not for myself, who will be for me? And when I am [only] for myself, what am I? And if not now, when?

Pirke Avot 1:14

Hillel's first question seems to imply that we have an obligation to look out for our own interests. Do you agree? Does this mean that we are perfectly justified in placing our own interests above those of others? In sacrificing other people's rights and needs to our own? In lying, cheating, or stealing in order to get what we want? What specific attitude does Hillel's second question warn against? What is the relationship between Hillel's third question and the first two?

Reproving, rebuking, accepting

The first ethical dilemma Paul has to resolve is whether to make use of the exam questions Milt and Larry have stolen. But even if Paul decides not to look at the questions, his ethical problems do not stop there. What obligation, if any, does Paul have to try to make his friends change their behavior? Should Paul keep silent about what he knows? Or should he tell his classmates? The teacher? Other school authorities? His friends' parents?

Reprove your neighbor, but incur no guilt because of him. . . . Love your neighbor as yourself.

Leviticus 19:17f

Do not follow a multitude [or, the majority] to do wrong.

Exodus 23:2

Should Paul try to persuade Milt and Larry to tell the teacher what they have done? What arguments might he use? Are they likely to be successful? What should Paul say if Milt tells him that "everybody's doing it" and that cheating has been going on in that class all year? Suppose Milt justifies sneaking a peak at the exam by complaining that this particular teacher gives trick questions. What should Paul answer?

When one sees anyone committing a crime or going on an evil path, it is his duty to cause him to improve by convincing him that he is committing a crime with his evil deeds, for it is said: "You shall surely rebuke your neighbor" (Leviticus 19:17). And . . . he must rebuke him in private, and he must speak to him quietly and use soft language, and should convince him that he is doing it only for his own good. . . . He who has the opportunity to prevent the commission of a crime and does not do so, will be caught with this crime himself.

S. Ganzfried, Code of Jewish Law *(Hebrew Publishing Co., 1927), 1:95f.*

How realistic is this advice from the Shulḥan Arukh? Suppose you and a friend were at a convenience store and you saw her put a pack of breath mints into her purse without paying for it. Would you say something to her before the two of you passed through the checkout counter? After you left the store? How might you tactfully and privately persuade her that what she did was wrong? What would you say if she told you to mind your own business and refused to put the breath mints back? Suppose she justified her theft by complaining that the manufacturer charged too much for the product, or that a big company wouldn't miss one roll of breath mints, or that the same store had ripped her off last week. What answer would you give her?

The passage seems to be saying that if you have the opportunity to prevent someone from committing a crime and fail to do so, you are as guilty as the original wrongdoer. Do you agree? If not, why not?

Squealers and whistle-blowers

If Paul is unable to persuade his friends to change their behavior, does he have an obligation to report the theft to school authorities? In answering this question, you may want to evaluate several additional factors. Will Milt and Larry know that it was Paul who informed on them? What is their response likely to be? Does Paul have reason to believe that the school will treat Milt and Larry fairly? Does the school have an honor code or pledge that all students must sign, signaling their willingness both to behave honestly and to report any cases of cheating? Were students involved in developing and implementing the honor code? How will school authorities react if they discover that students are no longer willing to abide by an honor system?

What might be a good reason for informing on someone else? A bad reason? How can you reconcile your desire to be loyal to your friends with the need to stand up for the truth?

In general, do you think honor codes and student honor boards are a good idea? Are students more likely to behave responsibly if they have a role in developing their own code of conduct? Do you know of cases in which other students cheated on an exam? What did you do when you found out?

The use of terms like *tattletale*, *squealer*, *blabbermouth*, *fink*, and *narc* suggests that society often takes a negative view of informers. But this is not always the case. In industry and government, someone who informs the outside world about waste, fraud, or corruption is called a *whistle-blower*. Laws exist to protect whistle-blowers from being punished by their employers or supervisors.

What might be a good reason for informing on someone else? A bad reason? Whose story are you more likely to trust: someone who stands up for honesty and the public interest, or an informer who seems primarily interested in protecting or enhancing his own position?

This section began with a discussion of whether Paul should voluntarily inform school authorities about the cheating scheme. But such disclosures are not always voluntary. Suppose the teacher calls Paul in to tell him she suspects Milt of having stolen the exam questions. If Paul will confirm her suspicions, she will absolve him. If she confirms it without Paul's cooperation, both he and Milt will be expelled from school. What should Paul do?

If two men are traveling in the desert and one has a flask of water, if both drink they will die. If only one drinks, he can reach civilization. The son of Patura taught: "It is better that both should drink and die, rather than that one should behold his companion's death." Rabbi Akiba taught: "'That your brother may live with you' (Leviticus 25:35) means your life takes precedence over his."

Baba Metzia 62a

What might the son of Patura have told Paul to do? What might Rabbi Akiba have answered? Who do you think was right?

Do people who are cheated deserve what they get? What steps, if any, should society take to prevent some people from taking advantage of others?

A game of "three-card monte" on the streets of New York.

Speculators on the London stock exchange (1720).

Ill-gotten gains

A Ḥasidic story tells of a Torah scroll in which an error was discovered. Since the Torah must be perfect in order to be read in the synagogue, the entire parchment panel was removed; all the material it contained was then laboriously rewritten and the new panel sewn into the scroll. When that portion was reached the following year, lo and behold, the identical error was found.

Amazed and upset, the rabbi ordered that the same procedure be repeated. But each time the panel was rewritten and replaced, the same error mysteriously reappeared. The story concludes by saying that when the case was thoroughly investigated, it turned out that the original donor of the Torah scroll had earned his money dishonestly. No gift from such a person could ever be usable in the synagogue.

[I]t is forbidden to derive any benefit from a notorious thief or robber . . . all of whose property is presumed to be either stolen or robbed. The poor are forbidden to accept a thief's money as charity.

Ganzfried, ibid., *4:73*

Suppose a man widely reputed to have made hundreds of millions of dollars through illegal arms sales wanted to donate $1 million to establish a food bank to feed the hungry and homeless. Should local authorities accept the offer? What impact would a decision not to accept the money have on the needy? What effect might a decision to accept the money have on the community at large?

Can we enjoy the benefits of great wealth, donated to worthy causes, without seeming to approve the way the money was originally accumulated?

John D. Rockefeller (1839–1937), who built his oil empire through ruthless business practices.

United Nations headquarters, built on land paid for with Rockefeller family money.

Many of the fortunes made through unfair business practices by the "robber barons" of the late nineteenth and early twentieth centuries later went to establish charitable foundations and to finance the construction of schools, libraries, and concert halls. How should we weigh the good some of these foundation gifts have done against the suffering that contributed to the accumulation of the original fortunes? Would we really be better off if cities and universities had refused to accept such donations? Is there any way the benefits of such contributions could be retained without seeming to condone the way this money was accumulated?

Scandal

Does Paul's case seem like fiction? Or like something that could happen only in school? On May 8, 1987, the *Boston Globe* reported that a U.S. District Court jury had convicted "six of the seven defendants accused in a scheme to steal and sell in advance copies of police promotional exams in one of the most widespread police corruption scandals in Massachusetts history." Who suffered when this police scandal was uncovered? Who would have been victimized if the cheating had not been exposed?

Take a quick glance at a daily newspaper or spend half an hour watching the nightly news and you'll see plenty of other scandals, including stories about the alleged bribe-taking, excessive drinking, and promiscuous sexual behavior of some of our most prominent political figures. Does the press have an obligation to report the personal failings of public officials? Is this information you feel you have a need or a right to know? To take one prominent example: to what extent, if any, do allegations that

John Kennedy was repeatedly unfaithful to his wife while in the White House affect your assessment of his performance as president?

In general, how large a role do you think questions of personal character should play in choosing political leaders? Do you regard such character questions as of greater, lesser, or equal importance to factors like competence, experience, political party affiliation, and stands on the issues? Do you think a candidate who would lie, cheat, or steal in his private life would be likely to do the same thing in public office?

Are there any limits to how far the press should go in gathering or reporting damaging information about people in public life? Do you think reporters have an obligation to take into account the feelings of the people they cover? If not, why not?

The whole truth?

Should we always tell the truth? The whole truth? Nothing but the truth? Always? Under all circumstances? Suppose your friend has just bought a new dress with earnings she has carefully accumulated over many months. She wears it for the first time and in great excitement asks how you like it. You think the dress is really ugly. Do you tell her so?

A more serious example: your aged grandfather is hospitalized with a life-threatening illness. His doctors are convinced that he will die shortly. Grandpa keeps asking what the doctors are saying. The family fears that to tell him the truth would destroy all his hope, increase his suffering, and probably hasten his death.

In Jewish tradition, truth has always been considered a very important virtue. In-

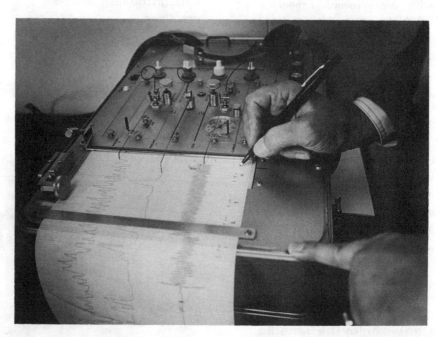

A polygraph machine, or lie detector.

Have you ever told the truth and later wished you had told a lie? Have you ever told a lie and later wished you had told the truth?

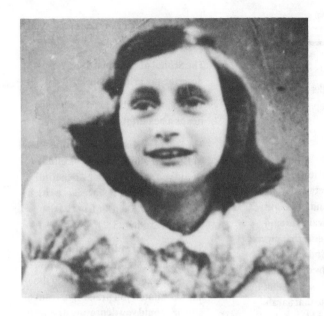

Anne Frank (1929–45).

The Anne Frank House in Amsterdam.

What would you have done to save Anne Frank? Would you have lied to protect her?

deed, we are told that TRUTH is one of God's names. Is it ever ethically permissible to deny or distort the truth? Could there conceivably be situations in which it would be more ethical to lie than to tell the truth?

Imagine yourself living in Holland during World War II. You live next door to the house where Anne Frank and her family are hiding, and you know they are there. A Nazi storm trooper questions you about people in your neighborhood who may be protecting Jews. Do you tell him the truth? Which is more ethical in this case, lying or telling the truth? How do we decide in any given instance?

The Ten Commandments

These are not easy questions to answer. It may help if we think for a moment of the Ten Commandments, the most important and impressive distillation of ethical guidelines humanity has ever devised. There is no commandment reading: "You shall not lie." Two commandments, however, do bear on the relation of truth to falsehood: "You shall not steal" and "You shall not bear false witness against your neighbor" (Exodus 20:13). These commandments disclose that lying is always wrong when it results in (a) stealing from others or (b) breaking a contract, which means destroying the kind of confidence and trust without which no orderly society or system of justice is possible.

What light do these standards shed on the following examples?

Elisha arrived in Damascus at a time when King Ben-hadad of Aram was ill. The king was told, "The man of God is on his way here," and he said to Hazael, "Take a gift with you and go meet the man of God, and through him inquire of the Lord: Will I recover from this illness?" Hazael went to meet him. . . . He came and stood before [Elisha] and said," . . . King Ben-hadad of Aram has sent me to you to ask, 'Will I recover from this illness?'" Elisha said to him, "Go and say to him, 'You will recover.' However, the Lord has revealed to me that he will die."

II Kings 8:7-10

Did Elisha lie? Did Elisha advise Hazael to lie? Why do you think Elisha counseled Hazael to tell the king he would recover?

It is permitted to tell a person who is seriously ill that he should turn his attention to his affairs. If he has lent money or deposited it with someone, or if others have lent him money or deposited their money with him, he should see that everything is in order. But he should be told that he need not fear that death is imminent because of these questions. . . .

When death draws near he is advised to confess. And we reassure him, "Many have confessed and then not died, just as many have not confessed and died. In the merit of your confessing you might be granted life."

Shulḥan Arukh, Yoreh De'ah *335:7, 338:1*

Under what circumstances does the Shulḥan Arukh advise telling the truth to a dying patient? Some doctors recommend that a patient should always be told the whole truth, others that this should never be done. How do you feel? To what extent does the answer to this question depend on the patient's mental ability and attitude? If you were seriously ill, how much would you want your doctor to tell you?

Sh'lom bayyit

According to our authorities, even God will hedge the truth in order to spare people's feelings and preserve domestic harmony.

The Talmud bases its doctrine of *sh'lom bayyit* [literally, peace at home] on a perceived discrepancy between what Sarah said of Abraham and what God reported to Abraham. Sarah had said, "How can I give birth, seeing that my husband is old?" When God speaks to Abraham, He puts it, "Why did Sarah ask, 'How can I give birth, seeing that I am old?'" The rabbis note that Sarah had attributed the age problem to her husband, but God "modified" her words. Had He reported them exactly, there would have been resentment of Sarah by Abraham; there would have been a loss of *sh'lom bayyit*. We learn from this that if even God, whose seal is Truth, can "modify" the story in order to preserve *sh'lom bayyit* between husband and wife, how much more should the rest of us modify and subordinate truth to peace, to peace between husband and wife; and between man and his fellowmen.

Rabbi David M. Feldman, Health and Medicine in the Jewish Tradition *(Crossroad, 1986), pp. 64f*

Our rabbis taught: How does one dance before the bride?

The School of Shammai says: You describe the bride as she is.

The School of Hillel says: You praise her as a beautiful and graceful bride.

The School of Shammai said to the School of Hillel: If she were lame or blind, would you still say of her, "Beautiful and graceful bride," since it is written in the Torah, "Keep far from a false matter" (Exodus 23:7)?

Said the School of Hillel to the School of Shammai: According to your view, if a person made a bad purchase in the market, should you praise it in front of him or should you deprecate it? Surely you should praise it!

Ketubot 16b, 17a

What justification is there, if any, for calling even a homely bride beautiful? What's the difference between that kind of lie and the kind Paul would be telling if he used the exam questions Milt and Larry stole? How can we distinguish between a lie which is justifiable and one which is indefensible?

Can you give an example of a lie you once told that you still think was ethically correct? Of a lie you thought was justifiable at the time, but which you now regret?

CHAPTER FOURTEEN

"I'M BEING TORN APART!"

Laura's problem

"I wish the rabbi would stop shooting his mouth off on things he really doesn't know anything about! I don't tell him how to teach Judaism. What gives him the right to tell me how to run my business?"

This wasn't the first time Laura Cohen had heard her father complain about their rabbi. But tonight, at dinner, he was so agitated she was afraid he would choke on his food. Nothing in the litany that followed her father's opening blast surprised her; she had heard it all many times.

The night before, Rabbi Fried had preached a sermon in support of the labor union that was threatening to strike Mr. Cohen's shoe factory.

"My dues help pay the rabbi's salary!" Laura's dad shouted. "How can he expect me to support the synagogue if he encourages the union to drive me out of

Few issues can so divide a community as a strike against a major employer. What role, if any, should the rabbi take in such a dispute?

business? And what does he know about running a business, anyway? He's never had to meet a payroll in his life. I have half a mind to resign from the congregation or start a movement to get rid of that rabbi!"

Laura complained one day to her best friend: "I'm being torn apart. My rabbi tells me one thing and my father insists the opposite is true. I want to be a good Jew and a loving daughter. How can I be both?"

Laura seems to be caught between two valid ethical ideals. One is the affection and respect that should prevail between parents and children. The other is the religious concern of Judaism to protect those who are disadvantaged and weak. What should Laura do? Here are several options:

1. Repudiate her father in anger, telling him he's not a good Jew and that she wants to have as little to do with him as possible.

2. Refuse to discuss these matters any further with her father. Adhere to her opinions but not voice them.

3. Explain to her father as patiently and respectfully as she can why she disagrees with him. Try without anger to convince him and ask that he respect her views, as she will honestly try to respect him.

4. Agree that because her father is older than she and probably wiser, he knows more and is probably right.

What would your advice be? Which similar options are available for Mr. Cohen and Rabbi Fried? Which would you recommend?

Rabbi and congregation

Do you think Rabbi Fried was right to offer public support to the workers in Mr. Cohen's factory? To what extent, if any, should a rabbi shape his sermons to reflect the views of the majority of his congregants? The views of the rabbinical organization to which he belongs? The policies of the United States government or Israeli leaders?

In general, do you believe rabbis should speak out on controversial economic, political, and social questions? Endorse particular candidates or political parties in election campaigns? Single out specific members of the congregation for criticism? Does the rabbi have any obligation to allow congregants who hold opposing views the opportunity to express them? You may want to address these same questions to your own rabbi.

Does a rabbi have the right to criticize the business practices of the very people who pay his salary? Do wealthy members of the congregation have the right to expect the rabbi to trim his views to match those of the temple's principal benefactors? What should members of the congregation do if they disagree with a position the rabbi takes? Keep their opinions to themselves? Argue with the rabbi privately? Demand equal time to express their own opinions? Threaten to withhold their annual dues? Try to get rid of the rabbi and find a new one? Resign from the temple and join—or start—a different congregation?

You may want to ask your parents, your teacher, or the rabbi whether any of the questions raised here have come up in your own synagogue. If so, how were they handled? Does your rabbi preach on political and economic issues? If so, how

do most members of the congregation and its governing board react? What do your parents think of such sermons?

Stephen S. Wise

Rabbi Fried is a product of my imagination. But there have been real rabbis very much like him.

Stephen S. Wise was one of them. In the fall of 1919 he preached a memorable sermon. Two things were at the center of his concern that day. The first was the building fund campaign his congregation had just announced, so they could worship in their own synagogue instead of a rented hall. The second was a strike the steelworkers' union in Pennsylvania had initiated against United States Steel, one of the largest corporations in the nation. Having just returned from visiting the steel mills, where he witnessed deplorable living and working conditions, Rabbi Wise was prepared to support the steelworkers in their demands.

In his sermon, Rabbi Wise told the congregation:

I know that there are penalties, many and grave, which are likely to attach themselves to this address. It is clear to me that there are scores of manufacturers, large and small, within the ranks of this congregation who may for a time in any event take serious objection to my thought. Some of them will doubtless determine to refuse to lend their help to the building of the Synagogue Home that has long been planned. I am ready to bear every burden and to pay every penalty. The one thing I am not ready to do is to conceal my inmost convictions. Better the truth spoken in

Stephen S. Wise (1874–1949).

Does a rabbi have the right to criticize the business practices of those who pay his salary? How should his congregants respond?

this hired meeting place, or in the littlest or humblest of meeting places, than concealment of conviction and evasion of truth in the most cathedral-like synagogue structure.

Before walking out onto the pulpit, Rabbi Wise had warned his wife, "Louise, my synagogue building is going up in smoke today." He was right. Many large donors, angered by his sermon, withdrew their building fund pledges, and the campaign had to be canceled. The congregation wasn't able to construct its synagogue until thirty years later. Rabbi Wise died before the building could be dedicated.

Compromise?

Rabbi Wise had to choose between his responsibility for the future of the congregation and his responsibility to teach and exemplify the values of Judaism, as he understood them. Do you think he made the right choice? Could he have found a way to fulfill both responsibilities at the same time? Suppose he had discussed his proposed sermon in advance with some of those whom he suspected it might offend. Do you think this might have helped reduce the negative reaction his sermon triggered? In delivering his sermon, do you think Rabbi Wise might have been somewhat less aggressive in his language without surrendering his ideals?

Consider now the fictional example of Rabbi Fried. Suppose he had sought out Mr. Cohen privately, or held a seminar for business and labor leaders in his congregation on the theme "What Judaism

Teaches About Business Ethics"? Would such tactics have helped to mollify Mr. Cohen's anger without sacrificing the principles Rabbi Fried held dear?

It might help—in other chapters as well as this one—to bear in mind that there are two types of compromise: those of principle and those of tactics or timing. In the first kind of compromise, where we trim an important value or ideal, we risk nibbling away at our goal until not enough is left to justify further struggle. In the second kind of compromise, where we focus on means rather than ends, we risk choosing expediency over ideals, so that in the end we justify doing nothing. It is often extremely difficult to determine how to achieve our ethical objectives in gradual stages (without ever forgetting the final purposes we hope to achieve), instead of pushing so hard and arousing so much intense opposition that we end up accomplishing nothing.

Judaism's social message

What did our ancestors teach about the rights of the poor? How did they weigh the need for a merchant to make a reasonable profit against the consumer's need for a good product at a fair price?

Listen to this, you who devour the needy, annihilating the poor of the land, saying, "If only the new moon were over so that we could sell grain; the sabbath, so that we could offer wheat for sale, using an *ephah* that is too small, and a *shekel* that is too big, tilting a dishonest scale, and selling grain refuse as grain! We will buy the poor for silver,

You shall not steal; you shall not deal deceitfully or falsely with one another. . . .

The wages of a laborer shall not remain with you until morning. . . .

You shall not falsify measures of length, weight, or capacity. You shall have an honest balance, honest weights, an honest *ephah*, an honest *hin*.

Leviticus 19:11-36

Why do you suppose the authors of Leviticus condemned the practice of not paying a worker promptly when the day's work was done? Some people say that honesty in business is not only right, it's also "good business." Do you agree? Does knowing that a firm deals fairly with its employees and honestly with its customers make you more or less likely to patronize that company?

Out of fear that defective weights and measures would be used and cause false weighing and measuring, the *mere possession* of faulty weights and measures is prohibited, even if held outside the marketplace.

Aaron Levine, Free Enterprise and Jewish Law *(Yeshiva University Press, 1980), p. 117*

Some economists and political theorists contend that businesses should be allowed to regulate themselves and that the free market alone should decide which companies prosper and which ones fail. Do you agree? How would our ancient authorities have responded to this argument?

Which unethical business practices did the prophet Amos condemn? To what extent can these abuses still be seen today?

the needy for a pair of sandals." The Lord swears by the Pride of Jacob: "I will never forget any of their doings."

Amos 8:4-7

Describe in your own words the business practices the prophet Amos condemned. How many of these practices are considered unethical or illegal by today's standards? Have any become accepted business practice? How do you suppose the merchants of Amos's own time reacted to his criticisms? How do businesses today respond to criticisms by governmental agencies and consumer groups?

The rights of workers

He who withholds a worker's wages is as though he deprived him of his life.
Baba Metzia 112a

The right of workers to form and join trade unions for the protection of their interests is also recognized in talmudical law. The rule that townspeople may

regulate prices, weights, measures, and wages . . . was extended to authorize the members of a given trade to fix hours and places of work and minimum or maximum wages for their trade. . . .

Haim H. Cohn, Human Rights in Jewish Law *(Ktav, 1984), pp. 101f*

If a person hires workers and asks them to work in the early morning or late evening, at a place where it is not the local custom to work early or late at night, he cannot force them to do so. If it is customary to provide food for workers, he must do so. If it is customary to give them dessert, he must do so—it all depends on local custom.

Mishnah Baba Metzia 7:1

Of course, our authorities recognized that workers had responsibilities as well as rights. Notice, for example, what the rabbis had to say about the now common practice of holding a second job, or "moonlighting." Why do you think the rabbis felt as they did? Do you agree?

A worker must not work at night at his own work and then hire himself out during the day; not plow with his cow in the evenings and hire her out in the mornings; nor should he go hungry and afflict himself in order to feed his children—for by doing so he steals labor from his employer.

Tosefta Baba Metzia 8:2

Just as the employer is enjoined not to deprive the poor worker of his wages or to withhold them from him when they are due, so the worker is enjoined not to deprive the employer of the benefit of his work by idling away his time, a little here and a little there, thus wasting the whole day deceitfully. . . . Indeed, the worker must be very punctual in the matter of time.

Maimonides, Mishneh Torah, "Laws Concerning Hiring," 13:7

A fire at the Triangle Shirtwaist factory in New York City in 1911 exposed the sweatshop's terrible working conditions.

Jewish labor leader David Dubinsky (1892–1982) headed the International Ladies' Garment Workers' Union for thirty-four years.

What does Jewish tradition say about the rights of workers? The responsibilities of employers?

What responsibilities do workers have to those who employ them? Which practices by workers does our tradition condemn?

Which of the following proposals and practices do you favor? Which do you oppose? Which seem to be most consistent with the spirit of Jewish tradition? Why?

■ Raising the minimum wage for all workers.

■ Compulsory health insurance for all workers.

■ Laws that restrict the power of unions to call strikes or organize boycotts.

■ Laws requiring employers to hire a certain percentage of minority applicants and women.

■ The use of lie-detector tests in employment interviews.

■ Compulsory drug testing for some employees, such as airplane pilots.

■ Compulsory drug testing for all employees.

■ Taking a second job on the night shift in order to have enough money to send a child to college.

The rights of consumers

Scripture says: "You have made humanity like the fish of the sea, like creeping things that have no rule" (Habakkuk 1:14).

Why are people compared to the fish of the sea?

Just as among the fish of the sea the larger ones swallow the smaller ones, so it is with people. If it were not for the fear of government, the stronger would swallow the weaker.

Avodah Zarah 4a

Do you agree with this last sentence? Do you believe the strong exploit the weak? If not, what prevents them from doing so? Do you believe that government officials more often side with the poor or with the powerful? With consumers or with business?

Judaism's concern for the subsistence needs of the masses finds expression in the rabbinical ordinance requiring each Jewish community to enforce a profit-rate limitation of one sixth for vendors dealing in commodities essential to human life.

Levine, ibid., p. 91

Jewish tradition supports controls not only on prices and profits but also on advertising and packaging.

Coloring of merchandise to give it an artificial appearance of freshness or better quality is forbidden. It is similarly forbidden to cover fruit of an inferior grade with a top layer of fruit of a higher quality. This is true even if the price is not raised as a result of the deception, which is used merely to attract the attention of buyers. . . .

A. P. Bloch, A Book of Jewish Ethical Concepts (Ktav, 1984), p. 121

One must be most careful not to cheat one's neighbor, whether he is a seller or a buyer. If one has something to sell, he is forbidden to make it look better than it really is, in order to deceive the customer.

Shulḥan Arukh

Which of the following practices do you feel are consistent with the spirit of Jewish ethics? Which are not?

- Before selling your house, you paint the outside to make it look more attractive.

- Before selling your car, you take it to a garage to have it tested and serviced.

- A restaurant owner advertises as "fresh-cooked" foods that were actually frozen and then heated in a microwave oven.

- An automobile company raises its prices by 10 percent to cover the cost of an extended warranty and a toll-free help line. The car is not changed in any way.

- An appliance store advertises a very low price for a stereo system. When you come into the store, the sales clerk tells you the advertised unit is really inferior to another unit that sells for a higher price and urges you to buy the more costly item.

- A toothpaste company changes the label from "Family Size" to "New Family Size" while reducing the contents by one-half ounce. The price remains the same.

- A supermarket raises the price of canned peas by 27 cents. It then advertises in the local newspaper a coupon offering "30 cents off" for the same can of peas.

What protection did Jewish tradition offer consumers? Which common marketing practices are specifically forbidden by Jewish law?

Supply and demand

Unlike some of today's economists, our ancestors did not consider increased demand a good reason for raising prices if the item sold was not changed in any way.

The law of the Torah prohibits the use on Passover of every type of ḥametz. . . .

Rab . . . said: "Earthenware pots in which leaven is cooked, and which absorbed and retained some of it, must be broken on Passover."

The sellers of new pots saw a chance to enrich themselves during the Passover season when the demand for fresh pots would be great; the harassed housewife would have been forced to pay unreasonable prices. But Samuel told these merchants: "Unless you charge an equitable price for your pots, I shall decide in accordance with Rabbi Simeon who permits the use of such pots after Passover. Then people will not break their pots before Passover . . . and you will find yourselves abundantly overstocked." **As Chief Justice and leading Rabbi of his day, Samuel had the power, in times of emergency, to ignore local law in order to uphold justice and fair prices. There was a buyer's market on the pot exchange that year and for a long time to come.**

M. M. Kellner (ed.), Contemporary Jewish Ethics (Sanhedrin Jewish Studies, 1978), pp. 336f

Do you agree with Samuel's decision? If not, why not? How would you respond to someone who argued that although Samuel's decision may have been right for his own time, it would mean disaster for today's world economy?

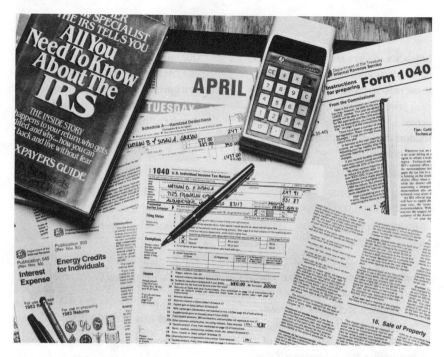

Stealing

People who would never dream of actually robbing someone else sometimes justify other kinds of stealing. At the dinner table, or in other conversations with your parents and their friends, you may have heard someone brag about underpaying income taxes, evading a traffic ticket, or "beating the system" in some other way. The idea usually is that a big company—or the government—can afford to take the loss. "They're always ripping us off," the reasoning goes. "Why shouldn't we come out ahead for a change?"

This was not the way our ancestors thought.

You must not steal, even if it be done merely to annoy, or even to restore double or fourfold or fivefold. Ben Bag Bag said: "You must not steal your own property back from a thief, lest you appear to be stealing."

Sifra 38b

One who robs the public [the many] must restore to the many. Worse is stealing from the many than stealing from an individual, for one who steals from an

Do taxpayers ever have the right to pay less in taxes than federal or state law requires? Can we justify tax evasion by citing our disagreement with a specific government policy, the fact that many government projects waste taxpayers' money, or revelations that some major companies pay no tax at all?

individual can appease that individual and return the theft; the former cannot.

Tosefta Baba Kamma 10:14

The operative principle governing payment of taxes is . . . , "The law of the government is the law." . . . [T]he Talmud . . . concludes that . . . deceiving the tax collector in any way is forbidden.

Kellner, ibid., *p. 344*

Suppose you discover that a drug store clerk has given you 35 cents more than you should have received in change. Would you give it back? Suppose she gave you ten dollars too much: how would that affect your decision? Would the knowledge that any loss will be deducted from her paycheck alter your behavior in any way?

A friend receives, incorrectly, a $240 check from an insurance company. He tells you: "Look, this is a big company which has overcharged me and many others for years. The extra money they sent me just corrects the balance a little." How do you respond?

Confessions

One of the most important and impressive of our High Holy Day prayers is *Al Ḥayt,* which we recite on Yom Kippur. In *Al Ḥayt,* we ask God to forgive us for all the sins we have committed, whether under duress or by choice, consciously or unconsciously, openly or secretly. A modern adaptation of *Al Ḥayt* reads this way:

For the sin we have committed by false advertising.
And for the sin we have committed by ruthless competition,

What ethical lessons, if any, can we learn from the games we play? To what extent do the rules, goals, and tactics of Monopoly and other business strategy games reflect or diverge from the teachings of Jewish tradition?

For the sin we have committed by manufacturing and selling inferior goods

And for the sin we have committed by putting property and profit ahead of human welfare,

For the sin we have committed by practicing deceit toward others, turning it into financial advantage for ourselves.

And for the sin we have committed by remaining silent in the face of evil,

For the sin we have committed by not helping the unemployed to find labor, thus depriving them of self-respect

And for the sin we have committed by contaminating our business and professional transactions with personal greed,

For the sin we have committed by resisting social change which would benefit the majority of our fellow-citizens, only because it might diminish our own material possessions.

And for the sin we have committed when, by innuendo or insinuation, we devalue another person's good name, . . .

For all these sins, O God of forgiveness, Forgive us, pardon us, grant us atonement.

Adapted by Mrs. Aron O. Lurie and Rabbi Roland Gittelsohn from Yearnings *(Rabbinical Assembly, 1968).*

How effectively does this revised version of *Al Ḥayt* address contemporary questions of business ethics? Can you think of any other unethical or illegal business practices that should have been included? Some congregants objected to the new version of *Al Ḥayt* by protesting that they personally had not been guilty of all the sins listed. How would you respond to them?

Endings

CHAPTER FIFTEEN

WHY ME?

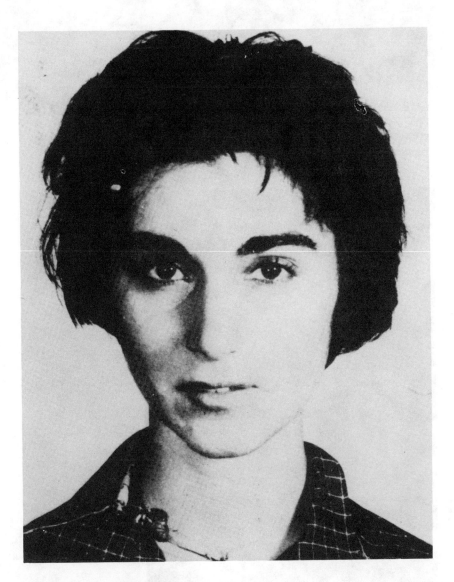

Would you have found a way to help Kitty Genovese? Or would you have found some reason not to become involved?

The Kitty Genovese case

At about 3:20 A.M. on March 13, 1964, in the residential neighborhood of Kew Gardens in New York City, a 28-year-old woman named Kitty Genovese was attacked by a man with a knife. Subsequent investigation revealed that during the next thirty minutes, at least 37 people who heard her screams and witnessed the fatal assault failed to come to her rescue—or even to call the police. Not until 3:50 A.M. did the police receive the first report from an eyewitness. By that time, Kitty Genovese had bled to death.

If you had been awakened in the middle of the night by a woman's screams, had looked out your bedroom window and seen Kitty Genovese being attacked—what would you have done? Screamed from the window to frighten away the attacker? Called the police? Summoned an ambulance? Rushed out on your own to help the victim? Tried to get other people in the neighborhood to come to Kitty's aid?

When interviewed by the police and by newspaper reporters, those who heard Kitty's screams but did nothing gave the following reasons for their inaction:

- I was afraid the assailant might attack me.

- I thought it was only a prank or an innocent scuffle.

- I didn't want to become involved.

- I didn't want the bother of having to appear as a witness in court.

- I feared that if I testified against the assailant, friends of his might harm me, too.

Which of these explanations seem convincing to you? Which sound like flimsy excuses?

Have you ever been in a situation similar to the one faced by Kitty Genovese's neighbors? How did you react? What did you do? In hindsight, do you think what you did was appropriate, insufficient, or possibly too risky?

Saving a life

How do we know that if you see someone drowning in a river, or attacked by bandits or a wild beast, you are obligated to come to his rescue, even at the cost of the attacker's life? Because it is written: "Do not stand idly by the blood of your neighbor."

Sifra, Leviticus 19:16

Notice that this rabbinic passage based on Leviticus says you are obligated to come to someone's rescue "even at the cost of the attacker's life"—not at the

Contrast the response of Reba and Jessica McClure's neighbors with Kitty Genovese's. How can you account for the difference? How can we build the kind of community where people care about and are willing to help one another?

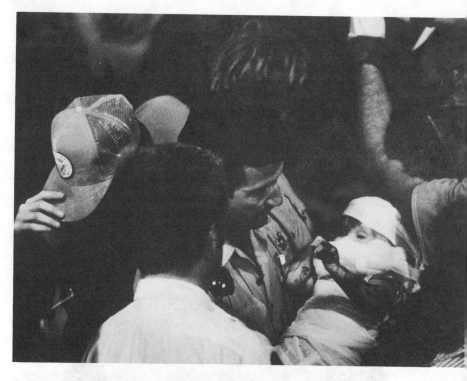

A rescue worker in Midland, Texas, holds eighteen-month-old Jessica McClure after she was pulled from an abandoned well.

Jessica's mother, Reba Gayle McClure, anxiously watching the rescue effort.

cost of your own. How can we balance the obligation to rescue against the possible risk to the rescuer?

Obviously, the duty of rescuing people in danger entails some risk to the rescuer. Nevertheless, that does not relieve one of his obligation, unless his own life would thereby be placed in jeopardy. A nonswimmer need not attempt life-saving because he would sacrifice his life in vain (Sefer Chasidim 674). Furthermore, there is no moral imperative to give one's life in order to save the life of another.

A. P. Bloch, A Book of Jewish Ethical Concepts *(Ktav, 1984), p. 259*

If one person is able to save another and does not save him, he transgresses the commandment, "Do not stand idly by the blood of your neighbor."

Similarly, if one person sees another drowning in the sea, or being attacked by bandits, or being attacked by wild animals, and although able to rescue him either alone or by hiring others, does not rescue him; or if one hears heathens or informers plotting evil against another or laying a trap for him and does not call it to the other's attention and let him know; or if one knows that a heathen or a violent person is going to attack another and although able to appease him on behalf of the other and make him change his mind, he does not do so; or if one acts in any similar manner—he transgresses in each case the injunction, "Do not stand idly by the blood of your neighbor."

Maimonides, Laws Concerning Murder and the Preservation of Life, *chap. 1, secs. 14, 16*

In each of the following situations, doing the "right thing" involves some risk to the doer. Evaluate the risk in each case and decide whether you would (a) do nothing, (b) take direct action despite the risk, or (c) find a safer way to accomplish the proper goal.

■ You witness a murder for which the wrong man has been charged. The real murderer warns you that if you tell the truth on the witness stand, you'll be his next victim.

■ You're probably the best swimmer on the beach, but high tides have made the ocean currents very tricky. You hear someone caught in the tide calling for help about one hundred feet offshore.

■ As a high-ranking officer on an oil tanker, you have often seen your captain drunk. You fear that his impaired judgment may wreck the tanker and cause a serious oil spill. But if you report him to the oil company, you may have to admit that you and other crew members have often been his drinking buddies on board ship.

■ A spacecraft is about to leave the launching pad in weather colder than its rockets were designed to withstand. You inform the mission controller, who tells you that because of pressure from the White House, which wants the launch for political reasons, you have no choice but to keep your objections to yourself.

■ As an employee of a major defense contractor, you discover that your company is selling the air force shoddy aircraft parts at inflated prices. You tell your supervisor, who warns you that if you say anything to anyone else, you'll be fired.

In Arthur Miller's tragedy *All My Sons,* **why is the fighter pilot driven to commit suicide? How should individuals and companies that sell defective or overpriced equipment to the armed forces be punished?**

Deplorable conduct

One of the central characters in *All My Sons,* a famous play by Arthur Miller, is a young man whose brother was killed overseas when his fighter plane crashed. At the play's climax, the young man discovers that his brother actually committed suicide by deliberately crashing his plane. He explained in a note to his sweetheart, revealed by her only years later, that he was driven to this desperate act when he learned that many of his friends in the air force had lost their lives when their planes failed in combat because of faulty parts and that those parts had been manufactured and knowingly delivered to the military by his own father.

Why did the pilot brother in *All My Sons* take such a drastic and irrevocable step? What was he trying to accomplish? Could he have achieved his purpose in a better way? Might he have acted differently if the manufacturer of the defective parts had not been his own father?

Unfortunately, tragically, the underlying premise of *All My Sons* is far from

Arthur Miller (1915–).

fictional. There have been numerous reports—even admissions and convictions—of American manufacturers who wittingly delivered untested or defective components or weapons to our military forces. How can we account for such deplorable conduct? If proven guilty, how should such individuals and companies be punished? Does their behavior differ in degree from that of inspectors on automobile assembly lines who fail to stop cars with faulty parts from being sold to the public? From the conduct of those who produce and sell cigarettes, causing disabling illness and death to smokers? What is your personal responsibility in such matters?

Whoever can prevent members of his household from committing a sin, but does not, is punished for the sins of his household.

If he can prevent his fellow citizens from committing sins, but does not, he is punished for the sins of his fellow citizens.

If he can prevent the whole world from committing sins, but does not, he is punished for the sins of the whole world.

Shabbat 54b

High school dilemmas

1. Rose, a high school junior, has overheard friends plotting to steal money from their class treasury; they plan to alter the record books in order to keep the theft secret. What should Rose do? Does she have any responsibility at all? Should she try to persuade her friends to abandon their plan? Report them to a teacher? To the police? Keep silent in order to retain their friendship?

2. With Rose, Len attends a predominantly white suburban school. For three years the county authorities, in an effort to desegregate the schools, have transported some forty black students daily from their inner-city homes to the suburbs. There has been little social contact, however, between the black and white students.

Despite this, Len has become friendly with Malcolm, a personable, intelligent, and talented black student in his class. He would like to propose Mal for membership in the extracurricular social club to which he belongs. But he fears that such a proposal would be opposed by many, perhaps most of the other members. His white friends have hinted, not too subtly, that his own membership might be in jeopardy if he continues to be seen with Mal.

What should Len and Malcolm do? Is Len helping or hurting Mal by pushing him for membership in the club? If Mal is refused admission, should Len resign in protest? What, if anything, can Len and Mal do to improve the overall climate of race relations at their school?

3. Len learns that some white students are planning to throw rocks at the bus that transports the inner-city students to and from school. They hope thereby not only to frighten the blacks, but also to persuade civic and school authorities that their integration plan should be abandoned.

Should Len tell Mal about the rock-throwing plot? Reveal it to his teachers? To school administrators? To the police? Try to dissuade the plotters? Just keep quiet for his own status and security?

To me, O Israelites, you are Just like the Ethiopians. True, I brought Israel up From the land of Egypt, But also the Philistines from Caphtor And the Arameans from Kir. Behold, the Lord God has His eye Upon the sinful kingdom: I will wipe it off The face of the earth!

Amos 9:7-8

What message do you think Amos holds for those who believe one race is superior to another? For those who think they have God "on their side"? What advice do you think Amos might give Len? Write a few lines, similar in style to those above, which you think the prophet might have penned in this situation. What might Amos's final threat mean to a person who doesn't believe in God?

Whites demonstrate against the busing of black children to a predominantly white school in New York City.

Court-ordered busing in Boston.

Blacks march for equal rights in Selma, Alabama.

What can you do to improve race relations in your school? In your community? In the nation as a whole?

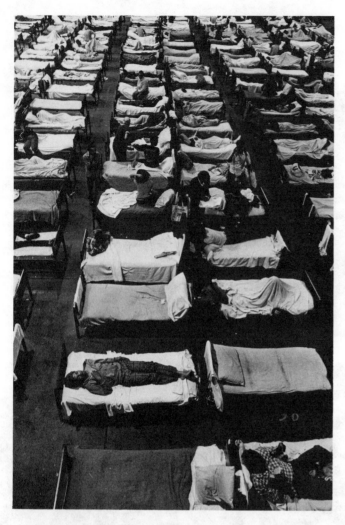

A shelter for the homeless
in New York City.

A homeless man in Wash-
ington, D.C.

A mother and child at Gra-
mercy Place, a halfway house
for the homeless operated by
the Jewish Federation in Los
Angeles.

A woman who has worked
diligently on behalf of Boston's homeless said,
"When I feed those who are
hungry, I'm called a saint.
When I ask *why* they are
hungry, I'm called a Com-
munist." What was she
really saying?

Helping the homeless

In recent sessions of their social studies class, both Len and Rose have been exposed to the problems of the homeless in their city. Among the questions they have explored is whether this is a situation for which they share personal responsibility or whether, instead, caring for the homeless is the obligation of society at large. Together with their classmates, they have outlined several proposals:

- Contribute money and labor to support a soup kitchen at which the hungry and homeless will receive daily meals.

- Invite the homeless for a Thanksgiving dinner or seder.

- "Adopt" one homeless family and try to raise funds to provide for their food, health, and educational needs.

- Rent a bus to demonstrate in Washington, D.C., in favor of low-rent housing construction.

- Organize a boycott of banks that are known to discriminate against minority applicants for home mortgage loans.

- Gather petitions in favor of a tax reform plan that would partially redistribute income, giving a larger proportion of the nation's wealth to the poor.

- Organize a traveling band to perform concerts and plays at shelters for the homeless.

Which activities do you think would be most effective? Least effective? In evaluating each proposal, try to weigh the advantages of personal action (e.g., volunteering in a soup kitchen) versus political action (e.g., lobbying the White House and Congress). Which offers the greatest personal satisfaction? The greatest opportunity for long-range success? The greatest likelihood of helping those who need help most?

What is your responsibility for helping the homeless? What can your class do?

Everyone's obligation

The story is told of a little French town whose inhabitants wanted to honor their physician, who was about to retire after faithfully guarding their health for many years. Knowing that he loved good wine, they decided to surprise him with a group gift. Each citizen was to bring a quart of his or her very best vintage, depositing it in a huge barrel that would be publicly presented to their beloved doctor. He was moved to tears by the mayor's emotional speech in presenting him with the gift. But when the doctor tapped the cask to taste the wonderful wine it contained, he discovered that it held only water. What had happened was immediately apparent to all the embarrassed townspeople. Each resident had figured that with so many other contributors donating their best wine, his own pitcher of water would never be discovered.

Why me? Why you? Why do *we* need to get involved when there are so many others to bear the responsibility?

During the German occupation of Denmark in the early 1940s, King Christian X, a vigorous foe of the Nazis, rode

Christian X (1870–1947), King of Denmark.

majestically through Copenhagen every morning on his horse, warmly greeting his people, contemptuously ignoring Hitler's troops. Did he thereby end the German occupation or inflict immediate injury on the Nazis? Of course not!

Yet it would be foolish to dismiss his behavior as futile bravado. Symbolically, he set an example that undoubtedly encouraged other Danes to conspire against the Nazis, to save untold numbers of Jewish refugees, to pave the way for the ultimate defeat of Hitler and his "final solution." Had the king and many others just asked "Why me?"—had they resorted to the easy excuse of saying that one or two individuals could do nothing to combat the monstrous and overpowering Nazi evil—German tyranny in Europe might never have been overthrown.

What would you have done in King Christian's place?

What made King Christian's daily horseback ride through the streets of Copenhagen an act of heroism? If you had been King of Denmark, what would you have done to combat the Nazis?

The balance

They ask Me for the right way,
They are eager for the nearness of God:
"Why, when we fasted, did You not see?
When we starved our bodies, did You
pay no heed?"
Because on your fast day
You see to your business
And oppress all your laborers!
Because you fast in strife and contention,
And you strike with a wicked fist! . . .
Is such the fast I desire,
A day for men to starve their bodies?
Is it bowing the head like a bulrush
And lying in sackcloth and ashes?
Do you call that a fast,

A day when the Lord is favorable?
No, this is the fast I desire:
To unlock the fetters of wickedness,
And untie the cords of the yoke.
To let the oppressed go free,
To break off every yoke.
It is to share your bread with the hungry,
And to take the wretched poor into your
home;
When you see the naked, to clothe him,
And not to ignore your own kin.

Isaiah 58:2-7

In this passage is Isaiah advising his
people not to fast on Yom Kippur? What
else do they need to do?

Our rabbis taught: Ever let a man see
himself as though he were half-guilty
and half-innocent. Happy is he if he
does one good deed, for he tips the
balance in his favor. Woe is he if he
commits one transgression, for he tips
the balance against him. . . .

Rabbi Eleazar ben Rabbi Simeon says:
Because the world is judged by its majority, and the individual judged by the
majority of his deeds, happy is the man
who does a single good deed, for he
tips the balance in his favor and that of
the world. Woe is he if he commits one
transgression, for he tips the balance
against himself and the world. For it is
said, "but one sinner destroys much
good" (Ecclesiastes 9:18). Because of a
single sin, he and all the world would
have lost much that is good.

Kiddushin 40b

What is the basic message of this passage? How does it answer the question
"Why me?"

CHAPTER SIXTEEN

ESPECIALLY ME!

Standards of conduct

Because of our unique ethical heritage, does the world expect more of Jews than of other peoples? Does the world apply higher standards of international conduct to the State of Israel than other nations are expected to meet? Do we Jews judge ourselves by higher standards than we judge non-Jews?

Although all religions teach about morality and justice, certainly our ancestors believed that Jews had some very special ethical obligations. Here is a parable attributed to the nineteenth-century Polish rabbi Jacob Kranz, who was popularly known as the Dubno Maggid, or just the Dubno.

Two thieves were once caught and brought before the judge. . . . One of the accused was found to have come from a father and grandfather who were themselves thieves, while the other's

How can we Jews live up to the highest standards of our remarkable ethical tradition? Do we expect more of ourselves than of other peoples? Should we?

forebears were, for several generations, noted rabbis and scholars. The judge gave a less severe sentence to the former than to the latter. Upon hearing the verdict, the second thief complained bitterly, "Why am I any worse than my companion? Why should I receive a more severe sentence than he?"

The judge replied: "Your companion came from a dishonest family, many of whom were thieves, and from their example he could learn nothing better than stealing. But you, whose father and grandfather were upright men, learned and scholarly, who set before you an exemplary path of honest living from which you broke away, definitely deserve a harsher punishment than your friend."

In like manner, implies the Dubno, God will say to Israel when judging them for their misdeeds: "You come from such fine origin; . . . [your ancestors] set such noble examples of good living for you to follow, but against which you rebelled and chose not to follow; you, therefore, more than the other nations who did not have such righteous ancestors, will be punished ever so severely by Me!"

Herman Glatt, He Spoke in Parables *(Jay Bithmar, 1957), pp. 153f*

Why did the judge punish one thief more harshly than the other? Why, according to the Dubno, does God impose a higher standard of conduct on Jews than on other peoples? Do you agree with the implications of this parable? Do you tend to judge people who come from "good" families more harshly than those who do not? Is it fair for someone to use religious heritage or family background as an excuse not to behave honestly and ethically toward others?

When non-Jews appear to expect a higher standard of ethical behavior from Israel and the Jews than from other nations and peoples, are they revealing latent anti-Semitism? When Jews express such expectations, are they demonstrating Jewish self-hatred?

What makes you feel special about being a Jew? Participating in Jewish rituals? Singing Jewish songs? Eating Jewish foods? Helping Israel or Soviet Jewry?

What makes you feel most special about being a Jew:

- Eating foods like bagels, matzah, and gefilte fish?

- Participating in such rituals as the Bar or Bat Mitzvah, Passover seder, and Shabbat services?

- Singing Jewish songs and enjoying Jewish literature, including the Hebrew Bible?

- Giving *tzedakah* to support the State of Israel, assist Soviet Jewry, or help the Jewish poor?

One of the words our teachers used to express the special quality of being Jewish is *holiness*. Thus, God spoke to our ancestors:

[Y]ou shall be to Me a kingdom of priests and a holy nation.

Exodus 19:6

What does holiness mean? In the beginning, holiness was marked by eating only special kinds of food or wearing distinctive apparel or living apart from others. Thus, in biblical times, nazirites were Jews who took special vows of holiness and were bound by particularly stringent regulations:

If anyone, man or woman, explicitly utters a nazirite's vow, to set himself apart for the Lord, he shall abstain from wine or ale . . . neither shall he drink anything in which grapes have been steeped, nor eat grapes, fresh or dried. . . .

Throughout the term of his own vow as nazirite, no razor shall touch his head. . . . Throughout the term that he has set apart for the Lord, he shall not go in where there is a dead person.

Numbers 6:2-6

The Holiness Code

Even prior to the close of the biblical period, our Jewish idea of holiness changed radically. The most eloquent expression of this newer concept of holiness appears in the nineteenth chapter of Leviticus, which is known as the Holiness Code:

The Lord spoke to Moses, saying: "Speak to the whole Israelite community and say to them:

You shall be holy, for I, the Lord your God, am holy.

You shall each revere his father and his mother, and keep my sabbaths: I the Lord am your God.

Do not turn to idols or make molten gods for yourselves: I the Lord am your God. . . .

When you reap the harvest of your land, you shall not reap all the way to the edges of your field, or gather the gleanings of your harvest. You shall not pick your vineyard bare, or gather the fallen fruit of your vineyard; you shall leave them for the poor and the stranger: I the Lord am your God.

You shall not steal; you shall not deal deceitfully or falsely with one another. You shall not swear falsely by My name, profaning the name of your God: I am the Lord.

You shall not coerce your neighbor. You shall not commit robbery. The wages of a laborer shall not remain with you until morning.

You shall not insult the deaf, or place a stumbling block before the blind. You shall revere your God: I am the Lord.

You shall not render an unfair decision: do not favor the poor or show deference to the rich; judge your neighbor fairly. Do not deal basely with your fellows. Do not profit by the blood of your neighbor: I am the Lord. . . .

Love your neighbor as yourself: I am the Lord.

Leviticus 19:1-18

How does the idea of holiness embodied in the Holiness Code differ from the concept of holiness practiced by the nazirites? Which concept has greater relevance for your daily life and conduct? Judged by the standards of the Holiness Code, could a nazirite who followed all the specific requirements of Numbers 6:2-6 still fail to be holy?

Judge each of the following examples of conduct by citing a specific provision of the Holiness Code that either approves or condemns it:

- A computer hacker creates a destructive "virus" and incorporates it into a program he distributes free to other computer users.

- Instead of throwing out its leftovers, a restaurant offers its excess food to a local soup kitchen.

- You duplicate an audiocassette by one of your favorite groups and sell it to a friend.

- Your school installs ramps and elevators to make its facilities more accessible to the handicapped.

- You tell the truth at an honor board hearing even though it means informing the investigators that your best friend was cheating.

- A clothing manufacturer reduces the price of its shirts sold in the United States by having them made in nations where wage rates and living standards are much lower than ours.

Holiness in everyday life

A modern Conservative rabbi has expressed his notion of holiness in an unusual way that builds on the Holiness Code and our other ethical literature. He suggests the following as a responsive reading for Kol Nidrei night:

Kol Nidrei is the holiest night of the year.
Many are the ways of holiness; varied are its paths.
   There is holiness in a lab when a vaccine is discovered to destroy diseases.
There is holiness when nations meet to beat swords into plowshares.
   There is holiness when people of different backgrounds work together for a common future.
There is holiness when people seek justice and struggle for righteousness.
   There is holiness when people lift up the fallen and free the captives.
There is holiness when people bring consolation to the sorrowing and comfort to the silent sufferers.
   There is holiness when people create lasting poetry or philosophy or song.
There is holiness when we strive to be true to the best we know.
   There is holiness when we are kind to someone who cannot possibly be of service to us.
There is holiness when we promote family harmony.
   There is holiness when we forget what divides us and remember what unites us.

In Jewish life, holiness can have many meanings: helping the poor, creating works of art, exploring the mysteries of the physical world, approaching God through meditation and prayer. What does holiness mean to you? When do you feel most holy?

There is holiness when we are willing to be laughed at for what we believe.

There is holiness when we love— truly, honestly, unselfishly.

There is holiness when we remember the lonely and bring cheer into a dark corner.

There is holiness when we share— our bread, our ideas, our enthusiasm.

There is holiness when we gather to pray to Him who gave us the power to pray.

Holy, holy, holy is the Lord of hosts; All of life can be filled with His glory.

Rabbi Sidney Greenberg

How valid do you find Rabbi Greenberg's expanded concept of holiness? Did any passages in his "holiness prayer" surprise you? Which provision, if any, would you omit? Which other examples of holiness might you add?

Chosen people, covenant people

Throughout our history we Jews have considered ourselves to be a special people, a chosen people. One expression of this conviction is in the first blessing we recite over the Torah:

Praised be the Lord our God, Ruling Spirit of the universe, who has chosen us from all peoples by giving us the Torah.

This theme recurs in several biblical declarations:

[Y]ou shall be my treasured possession among all the peoples.

Exodus 19:5

For you are a people consecrated to the Lord your God: of all the peoples on earth the Lord your God chose you to be a treasured people.

Deuteronomy 7:6

We also refer to ourselves frequently as a covenant people. This, too, comes from assurances given in the Bible.

You stand this day, all of you, before the Lord your God—your tribal heads, your elders and your officials, all the men of Israel, your children, your wives, even the stranger within your camp, from woodchopper to water drawer—to enter into the covenant of the Lord your God, which the Lord your God is concluding with you this day. . . . I make this covenant, with its sanctions, not with you alone, but both with those who are standing here with us this day before the Lord our God and with those who are not with us here this day.

Deuteronomy 29:9-14

What does "chosenness" mean? Does it mean that we Jews have been singled out for special privileges? That we are necessarily better than other peoples? If not, what does it mean? Who is included in the covenant? Is anyone excluded? According to Deuteronomy, can a Jew choose to be excluded from the covenant?

The meaning of the covenant

The dictionary gives *contract* and *agreement* as synonyms for the word *covenant*. Yet there is a difference among these terms. We trivialize the word *covenant* when we apply it to an agreement between you and your friend to meet at the corner drug store, or to a contract pledging one person to sell a house to another. The word

covenant really should be reserved for something more important, something sacred or holy. The marriage of two people who love each other enough to establish a permanent life partnership can properly be called a covenant. It enhances the lives of both, raising them to a higher dimension of experience than they could otherwise know.

Similarly, the relationship between our Jewish people and God is properly referred to as a covenant. If properly understood and adhered to, it enhances both partners. It makes us chosen and holy in more than just a pretentious way. Does it sound presumptuous to suggest that our taking the covenant seriously can also enhance God? Some of our ancient teachers would not have thought so. They were bold enough to say:

When the Israelites do God's will, they add to the power of God on high. When the Israelites do not do God's will, they, as it were, weaken the great power of God on high.

Pesikta 166a

"You are My witnesses, says the Lord, and I am God" (Isaiah 43:12). That is, when you are My witnesses I am God, and when you are not my witnesses I am, as it were, not God.

Pesikta 102b

How do you interpret these two passages? In what sense can it be said that when we do not do God's will, we diminish His power? How do you respond to the idea that when we do not act as God's witnesses, then God is "not God"?

A distinguished modern Jewish thinker, a professor at the Hebrew Union College-Jewish Institute of Religion, was even more radical and explicit in expressing the effect we can have if we fulfill our share of the covenant:

Maybe it is our task as human beings to be helpers and co-creators with a God who is still in process of gradual realization, who needs our strength to carry out His designs as we need His strength to hearten us. *Maybe God and perfection are at the end and not at the beginning*. Maybe it is a growing world and a growing mankind and a growing God, and perfection is to be achieved, and not something to start with.

Our own prophets and prayer books seem to have had an inkling of this fact. At culminating points in our liturgy we say in a phrase borrowed from one of

the last of the prophets (Zechariah 14:9): "On that day He shall be one and His name shall be one." On *that* day, not as yet alas, but surely on that day He shall be one *as He is not yet one*. For how can God be called one, i.e., real, if mankind is rent asunder in misery and poverty and hate and war? When mankind has achieved its own reality and unity, it will thereby have achieved God's reality and unity. Till then God is merely an idea, an ideal: the world's history consists in making that ideal real. In simple religious earnestness it can be said that God . . . *exists only in part, and is slowly being translated into reality*.

Henry Slonimsky, Essays (Hebrew Union College Press, 1967), pp. 123f

What do we mean when we call ourselves the chosen people? In what sense must we be a choosing people, too? How can you, as an individual Jew, be a participant in and witness to the Jewish people's covenant with God?

Would you characterize Slonimsky's view of our relationship with God as optimistic or pessimistic? In Slonimsky's view, which kinds of actions might serve to diminish God's existence? Which may help make God real? What obligations does his view of God impose on humanity in general? On Jews in particular?

A more prosaic way of making Slonimsky's point is to recognize that of all God's creatures, only we human beings are aware of God's existence. Without us, God would exist, so to speak, in a vacuum. No form of earthly life would even be aware of Him. Surely in this sense it is true to say that our covenantal relationship with God enhances God as well as ourselves.

Conditions

Like many contracts, our covenant with God is conditional—that is, we enjoy the benefits only if we live up to our responsibilities.

Now then, if you will obey Me faithfully and keep My covenant, you shall be My treasured possession among all the peoples.

Exodus 19:5

That *if* is enormously important! The same condition is repeated later in the Torah:

The Lord will establish you as His holy people, as He swore to you, if you keep the commandments of the Lord your God and walk in His ways.

Deuteronomy 28:9

Again, *if*! And what if we do not?

If not for the fact that you accepted My Torah, I would not have especially recognized you, nor would I consider you to be any better than idol worshippers.

Exodus Rabbah 47:3

It pleased the Holy One, praised be He, to grant merit to Israel; that is why He gave them Torah and commandments in abundance.

Pirke Avot 6:11

Perhaps the most emphatic and convincing negative statement of what chosenness really means in Jewish thought comes from the prophet Amos:

Hear this word, O people of Israel, That the Lord has spoken concerning you, Concerning the whole family that I brought up from Egypt: You alone have I singled out Of all the families of the earth— That is why I will call you to account For all your iniquities.

Amos 3:1-2

Notice the last two lines: not "that is why I especially favor you" or "that is why I grant you extra privileges," but "that is why I will call you to account for all your iniquities."

A more comforting connection between chosenness and holiness is drawn in the Book of Isaiah:

I the Lord, in My grace, have summoned you, And I have grasped you by the hand. I created you, and appointed you a A covenant people, a light of nations— Opening eyes deprived of light, Rescuing prisoners from confinement, From the dungeon those who sit in darkness. . . . It is too little that you should be My servant In that I raise up the tribes of Jacob And restore the survivors of Israel: I will also make you a light of nations, That My salvation may reach the ends of the earth.

Isaiah 42:6-7, 49:6

Fulfilling the Jewish mission

What effect, if any, do concepts like chosenness and holiness have on your personal behavior? On your sense of moral responsibility? Do you think that Jews today should act as though they were a "treasured possession" among all God's peoples? Do you think your own actions could serve as "a light of nations"? What changes would you need to make in your thinking and behavior in order to accomplish that goal?

Other peoples, too, have demonstrated a unique genius: the ancient Greeks in philosophy, literature, and art; the Romans in law; modern Americans in political democracy. In a way, all these peoples might also be called "chosen." How, in your own words, would you characterize our special Jewish genius? From what you know of other religions, such as Buddhism, Christianity, and Islam, how would you describe Judaism's distinctive way of looking at the world?

Many Jews consider the State of Israel to be a very special witness to the holiness of the Jewish people and our covenant with God. This is the one place on earth where we Jews control our own political and spiritual lives, where the principles and ideals of Judaism can be implemented to their fullest and applied both to individual lives and society. What aspects of life in Israel today do you consider to be examples of holiness? Of Jewish chosenness? In what ways does Israel today fall short of these ideals?

You

How can you, as an individual Jew, be a participant in and witness to the covenant between the Jewish people and God? What real difference does it make whether any one of us as an individual feels responsible for the covenant? Does it make any difference to God? To the world? To the Jewish people and our prospects for survival? To your mental health and happiness?

So we reach not the end but a resting place in our quest for guidance. The ethical issues we have considered in these pages—along with many others we haven't had time or space to raise—will concern us for the rest of our lives. Always there will be crises and questions, dilemmas and doubts, a need for direction and advice. Always we do well to consult the wisdom of our ancestors, not invariably to be bound by their decisions, but to understand their ways of thinking in order to develop our own.

Final judgment for each of us must rest within our own minds and hearts. Let us strive for the best judgment we can achieve, in the spirit of our ancestors who responded to Moses when he gave them the Law: *"Na-a-seh v'nishma*—we will observe; we will try to understand!"

GLOSSARY

AND GUIDE TO FURTHER STUDY

Akiba (c. 50–135 C.E.), outstanding scholar and teacher of the rabbinic period.

Amos 1. Hebrew prophet of the eighth century B.C.E. 2. The book of the Bible that bears his name.

Arakhin ("Valuations"), talmudic tractate that comments on Leviticus 27:1–34.

Avodah Zarah ("Idol Worship"), talmudic tractate dealing mainly with idolaters and idolatry.

Baba Batra ("Last Gate"), talmudic tractate dealing predominantly with property law.

Baba Kamma ("First Gate"), talmudic tractate dealing mainly with damages for which one person can sue another.

Baba Metzia ("Middle Gate"), talmudic tractate dealing primarily with civil law.

Babylonian Talmud; see Talmud.

Central Conference of American Rabbis, the national association of Reform rabbis, founded in 1889.

Chronicles, the last book of the Hebrew Bible; its two parts are usually called I Chronicles and II Chronicles.

Deuteronomy (from Greek, "Repetition of the Law"), the fifth book of the Bible; one of the Five Books of Moses.

Deuteronomy Rabbah, Midrash on the Book of Deuteronomy, probably compiled between the seventh and tenth centuries C.E.

Ecclesiastes (from Greek, "Convoker"), a book of the Bible; one of the Five Scrolls, traditionally read on Sukkot.

Ecclesiastes Rabbah, Midrash on the Book of Ecclesiastes, probably compiled between the seventh and tenth centuries C.E.

Eruvin ("Mixing"), talmudic tractate that deals mainly with Shabbat laws and practices.

Exodus (from Greek, "Departure"), the second book of the Bible; one of the Five Books of Moses.

Exodus Rabbah, Midrash on the Book of Exodus, probably compiled between the tenth and eleventh centuries C.E.

Ezra 1. Hebrew priest and scribe who lived during the fifth or fourth century B.C.E. 2. The book of the Bible that bears his name.

Genesis (from Greek, "Origin"), the first book of the Bible, one of the Five Books of Moses.

Genesis Rabbah, Midrash on the Book of Genesis, probably compiled during the fifth century C.E.

Habakkuk 1. Hebrew prophet who probably lived during the seventh century B.C.E. 2. The book of the Bible that bears his name.

Hillel (c. first century C.E.), one of the greatest and most beloved teachers of the rabbinic period.

Holiness Code, a section of Leviticus, especially chap. 19, embodying the Jewish ideal of holiness.

Iggeret Hakodesh ("Holy Letter"), a thirteenth-century Hebrew marriage manual.

Isaiah 1. Hebrew prophet who lived during the eighth century B.C.E. 2. The book of the Bible that bears his name.

Jerusalem Talmud: see Talmud.

Job 1. A biblical character who, in his affliction, challenges God to explain the meaning of suffering and the origins of evil. 2. The book of the Bible that bears his name.

Judges, the book of the Bible that covers the period in Israel's history between the death of Joshua and the establishment of the monarchy.

Ketubot ("Marriage Contracts"), talmudic tractate dealing with marriage contracts.

Kiddushin ("Betrothal"), talmudic tractate dealing mainly with prenuptial and marital arrangements.

Kings, the book of the Bible that covers the period from the death of David through the collapse of the Kingdom of Judah; its two parts are usually called I Kings and II Kings.

Leviticus (from Greek, "Of the Levites"), the third book of the Bible; one of the Five Books of Moses.

Leviticus Rabbah, Midrash on the Book of Leviticus, probably compiled during the fifth century C.E.

Maimonides, Moses (1135-1204 C.E.), great Jewish scholar, philosopher, physician, and communal leader; *see also* Mishneh Torah.

Midrash ("Investigation"). 1. A type of rabbinic literature that explains and amplifies the Bible, often through maxims and stories. 2. A collection of midrashic stories and sayings.

Midrash Aseret Hadibrot, a collection of stories probably compiled in the eleventh century C.E., dealing mainly with the Ten Commandments.

Mishnah ("Study"), sacred code of Jewish law compiled at Yavneh, in Eretz Yisrael, no later than 200 C.E.; part of the Talmud.

Mishneh Torah ("Repetition of the Law"), comprehensive Jewish law code compiled about 1180 C.E. by Moses Maimonides.

Mo'ed Katan ("Small Festival"), talmudic tractate dealing mainly with the intermediate days of festivals.

Nedarim ("Vows"), talmudic tractate based on Numbers 30 and dealing mainly with promises and obligations.

Numbers, the fourth book of the Bible; one of the Five Books of Moses.

Numbers Rabbah, Midrash on the Book of Numbers, probably compiled during the twelfth century C.E.

Peah ("Corner"), talmudic tractate based on Leviticus 19:9–10 and dealing mainly with obligations toward the poor.

Pesikta ("Portion"), Midrash probably compiled during the sixth or seventh centuries C.E.

Pirke Avot ("Chapters of the Fathers"), talmudic tractate that is a particularly rich source of ethical teachings.

Proverbs, a book of the Bible.

Psalms, a book of the Bible.

Rabbinical Assembly of America, the national organization of Conservative rabbis, founded in 1901.

Ruth 1. Biblical character who became a Jew-by-choice. 2. The book of the Bible that bears her name; one of the Five Scrolls, traditionally read on Shavuot.

Samuel, the book of the Bible that covers the period from the eleventh century B.C.E. through the kingships of Saul and David; its two parts are usually called I Samuel and II Samuel.

Sanhedrin ("Court of Justice"), talmudic tractate dealing mainly with judicial matters.

Semahot ("Rejoicings"), a collection of rabbinic writings on death and mourning, probably compiled between the fourth and eighth centuries C.E.

Shabbat, talmudic tractate that deals with the laws of Sabbath observance.

Shulhan Arukh ("Prepared Table"), a guide to Jewish law and practice compiled by Joseph Caro (1488–1575).

Sifra ("Book"), Midrash on the Book of Leviticus, probably compiled after the fourth century C.E.

Sotah ("Errant Wife"), talmudic tractate based on Numbers 5:11–31 and dealing mainly with adultery.

Talmud ("Instruction"), sacred books of Jewish practice compiled about 1500 years ago. The Jerusalem Talmud contains the Mishnah along with the commentaries of rabbinic authorities in Eretz Yisrael; the Babylonian Talmud supplements the Mishnah with commentaries by the rabbinic authorities of Babylonia.

Ta'anit ("Fast"), talmudic tractate dealing mainly with the regulations governing fasting.

Tanhuma on Genesis, Midrash on the Book of Genesis, compiled between the eighth and tenth centuries C.E.

Tosafot ("Additions"), collections of medieval commentaries on the Talmud.

Tosefta ("Additions"), supplements to the Mishnah probably compiled during the third century C.E.

tractate, a principal division of the Talmud.

Wisdom of Ben Sira, a collection of Hebrew proverbs and poems probably compiled during the second century C.E.

Yevamot ("Levirate Marriages"), talmudic tractate based on Deuteronomy 25:5–10 and dealing mainly with the ancient custom according to which a childless widow was expected to marry her late husband's brother.

Yoma ("The Day"), talmudic tractate dealing primarily with Yom Kippur.

Zohar Hadash ("New Splendor"), a collection of Hebrew texts compiled at Safed, in Eretz Yisrael, during the sixteenth century.

SUBJECT INDEX

HOW DO I DECIDE?

**A CONTEMPORARY JEWISH APPROACH
TO WHAT'S RIGHT AND WHAT'S WRONG**